THE BARONS
OF NEWPORT

Statues at Belcourt Castle

By Terrence Gavan

Cover photograph: *The Elms*. Photo courtesy of Preservation Societ·
County by Richard Cheek.
The author wishes to thank the Redwood Library for research

Published by Pineapple Publications
24 Bridge Street, Newport, RI 02840
(401) 847-0859

PRINTED BY SHANK PAINTER PRINTING COMPANY, PROVINCE1·

Table of Contents

Introduction 3

Newport—The American Capital of
    Conspicuous Consumption 4

Of Mansions and Madness..................10

The Gilded Playground....................18

Mrs. Astor—The Queen of Newport..........25

King Lehr—The Story of Harry and Bessie 29

The Great Triumvirate—
    Alva, Mamie, and Tessie 34

The Vanderbilts—Newport's First Family......43

Barons and Baronies 62

INTRODUCTION

They were heady times, those days between 1890 and 1914. It was the Gilded Age, the American Renaissance, and America was developing a national self-confidence and feeling her oats as an economic and political world power.

It was a time of opportunity, tremendous opportunity, particularly for accumulating wealth, as the federal income tax and anti-trust laws were a thing of the future.

Americans were gathering wealth at a frightening pace. In the middle of the 19th century there were only a few millionaires, but by the turn of the century there were a few thousand.

Much of this new wealth gravitated to Newport, Rhode Island, and the City by the Sea became the principal watering hole for a new class of aristocrats.

The Barons of Newport reveals the behavior of this remarkable group and illustrates the results of a lifestyle uninhibited by financial constraints.

In this story you'll meet a most incredible cast of characters, including the world's richest families, the Vanderbilts and the Astors. You'll follow prominent members of the elite and exalted Four Hundred, see their outrageous and extravagent lifestyles, and walk through their wondrous summer mansions.

As you read about the fabulous fortunes of the barons of Newport, it's important to note that their wealth was denominated in the turn-of-the-century dollar, a currency much more valuable than today's dollar. The equivalent buying power of a dollar in 1900 could be a hundred times greater than a dollar today. So a Gilded Age millionaire could be equal to today's hundred millionaire.

Most of the family dynasties of the Gilded Age have long since dispersed or withered, but most of Gilded Age Newport has been preserved. You can still view and even tour the fabulous mansions. You can stroll Cliff Walk and Bellevue Avenue, visit the Casino, and drive Ocean Drive (but you still can't get into Bailey's Beach). This book will help you plan your tour, find your way around, and, I hope, give you a sense of a society of extravagance and ostentation that will never be duplicated.

Terrence Gavan
Newport, Rhode Island

NEWPORT

The American Capital of Conspicuous Consumption

At the turn of the century, Newport was the social pinnacle, the epitome, the hands-down Mecca. Sure there were formidable pretenders — Palm Beach, Bar Harbor, Saratoga — but none could compare.

There were few doubters; Newport, Rhode Island, reigned supreme as the queen of American resorts from 1890 to 1914 (the Gilded Age).

During these glory days the absolute upper crust made Newport its summer headquarters. Newport was simply the place to be.

American society catapulted to world prominence during this era, and European royalty flocked to Newport to rub elbows with the social titans and fortune hunt among their debutantes.

This era saw the genesis of the American woman as a social and political force, and this force was ratified by the suffragette movement.

The deep pockets and strong will of Newport's Alva Vanderbilt Belmont were formidable ammunition in this struggle. She contributed heavily to the movement and sponsored a suffragette rally at her Bellevue Avenue mansion, Marble House. The emerging power of women was clearly evident in Newport society, and in more than just the suffragette movement.

Although men made the money and built industrial empires, it was the women who defined the new American social phenomenon of conspicuous consumption. In most cases the men were willing collaborators, but they generally lacked the time, talent, or interest in the daily minutia society demanded.

Gilded Age women of wealth, lacking the cultural license to engage in industrial empire building, were relegated by default to running households and filling time as they saw fit.

So they took what freedoms they had and parlayed them into a social juggernaut of extravagence and opulence. They created society with a capital "S" and in the process controlled immense power and wealth.

Newport was the arena for their social conficts, the catalyst for their extravagence, and the setting for their marriage brokering.

The dowagers and matrons of Newport had virtual carte blanche in the daily operation of their households (which they often ruled with an iron hand) and in the financing of their lavish and innovative affairs.

As much as men, if not more, women were the "Barons of Newport," and in this book, "Barons" is a genderless term.

EARLY PROSPERITY

Newport was famous on its own account long before the dawn of the Gilded Age.

A group of religious dissidents from the Massachusetts Bay Colony founded Newport in 1639. The progenitors of many eminent Newport families were in this group: Coddington, Easton, Coggeshall, Brenton, and Hazard. Through the industriousness and vision of these early colonists, Newport quickly achieved economic prominence and, during the early 1700s, ranked equally with New York, Boston, and Philadelphia.

Throughout the first half of the 1700s, the seaport flourished as an export center for shipbuilding, farming, and manufacturing of fine furniture and silverware. Newport became a supplier to other coastal colonies as well as the West Indies and Europe. The port city played a key role in the illicit but profitable "triangle trade," which involved exchanging rum, mollasses, and slaves between New England, the West Indies, and Africa. Many prominent merchants were engaged in the slave trade—a principal contributor to the growth of Newport's affluence.

Newport Waterfront, c. 1900

CULTURAL MAGNET

Increased propserity fostered development of the arts and trades. Architecture and carpentry thrived on the need for public buildings and homes for the affluent.

Many prominent travelers visited colonial Newport, and it became a principal gateway between the old and new worlds. Some of these visitors settled in the city and greatly enchanced the cultural atmosphere.

George Berkeley, a powerful figure in religion and literature, spent several years in Newport before returning to England.

An atmosphere of religious tolerance promoted the immigration of many persecuted minorities. Most notable were Quakers, Jews, and Baptists. The spirit of cooperation and diligence of these people contributed much to the city's economy. It also helped create a cultural center and a cosmopolitan society unrivaled in the New World.

Colonial Newport became a thriving tourist center. Summer visitors came from up and down the east coast and as far away as the Caribbean. Because of its strong maritime trade, Newport had a widespread reputation. The island was known for its healthful air and climate. Visitors from the south mixed well and had much in common with the agriculture and merchant families of Newport.

Newport is the best living example of American Colonial heritage. The City by the Sea probably has more original Colonial houses still standing than anywhere. Newport is famous for the oldest American synagogue (Touro), the oldest library (Redwood), and the first tavern (White Horse).

THE REVOLUTION

Colonial Newport's affluence and wealth soon attracted the attention of the British government. Perhaps it was greed, envy, or an exhausted treasury (the financial results of numerous wars with France and Spain), but the mother country began enforcing restrictive trade and maritime tax laws.

This led to several incidents during the late 1760s between the British Navy and Colonial rebels. Colonists burned customs ships in and around Newport harbor, and riots were widespread. The city population divided between loyalist and patriot.

The low point of Newport's history was a three-year period beginning in December 1776, when a British fleet landed with a force of 6000 troops. The tyrannical General Prescott commanded the British occupation force and made life as wretched as possible for the colonists who remained in Newport. Many prominent families, their lives in ruin, fled the city.

Eventually, the British ended their occupation upon news of an approaching French force. However, before their departure, the British looted the city, burned houses and wharves, and cut down nearly all the trees. This destroyed the economic vitality and cultural spirit of an already demoralized population. Newporters survived the approaching cold winter by ripping firewood from abandoned houses.

A mild renaissance occurred during the ensuing French occupation and restored much of the lost spirit and gaiety to Newport's soul. The gallant French officers led by General Rochambeau won the hearts of the people.

General George Washington met Rochambeau in Newport to plan the decisive battle of Yorktown.

TRANSITION PERIOD

After the revolution, Newport never again emerged as a dominant commercial force. Continuous maritime hostilities with England made trading difficult, as Newport was practically cut out of markets in the Caribbean. Later, with the advent of the railroad, the importance of maritime trade waned, and Newport's island isolation left it cut off from any land routes.

There was little activity in Newport during the early 1800s. Newporter Oliver Perry was famous in the War of 1812 for "damning the torpedoes" during the Battle of Lake Erie, and his brother Matthew Perry helped open trade with Japan. The Perrys were part of the roots of the rich naval tradition found in Newport.

By the middle of the 19th century, summer visitors began to trickle back into Newport. Slowly the city regained prominence as a tourist center. Hotels and inns flourished as resorters flocked to enjoy the healthful air and mild climate.

But the advent of the Civil War abruptly ended a budding summer migration of southern gentry, mostly wealthy planters.

After the war, a large and diverse group of New England intellectuals made Newport their summer retreat and served to renew the city's moribund cultural heritage.

Luminaries like Oliver Wendell Holmes, Henry Wadsworth Longfellow, Henry James, Julia Ward Howe, John Singer Sargent, and Edgar Allen Poe (one season) summered in Newport. Even Bret Harte livened several dinner parties during the summer of 1871.

This cultural cream, along with other wealthy Boston Brahmins, built stately but tasteful cottages, mostly on the hill near the center of the city. The area along lower Bellevue Avenue and Ochre Point was as yet only sparsely developed.

GILDED AGE

Suddenly the scene shifted. Late in the 19th century, Gilded Age millionaires, attracted by Newport's cultural reputation and the opportunity to mingle with the intelligentsia, descended in droves on the City by the Sea.

The elite (but snobbish in their own way) intellectuals wanted no part of this gaudy nouveau riche group. So, the intellectuals vacated Newport, inadvertently driven out by the new social invaders, and from then on, distinguished party guests like Bret Harte would be replaced by the likes of an Austrian archduke or an English polo champion.

Who were these people, where did they come from, and how did they get so rich?

Well, they were the Vanderbilts, the Astors, the Belmonts, the Fishes, the Havemeyers, the Goelets, the Berwinds, and hundreds more. They came from all over the country, but mostly from New York.

They got so rich by benefitting enormously from several phenomena like the Industrial Revolution, the Civil War (profiteering), lack of a federal income tax, abundant and cheap immigrant labor, and a combination of creativity and hard work with a dash of ruthlessness.

These nouveau riche with their sudden wealth often lacked the polish and grace required for aristocratic status. Their collective insecurity, supplemented by a restlessness for recognition, contributed greatly to the excesses of their lifestyles.

So, when they needed a summer retreat as a depository for their ostentation, they looked to Newport with its colonial heritage and understated patrician demeanor.

The Breakers, c. 1900

These Gilded Agers left an indelible imprint on the City by the Sea, as attested by their monumental mansions (some seemingly a cross between Grand Central Station and the Palace of Versailles).

Criticisms of this group ranged from silly to scandalous to insensitive to immoral. Across the country, from editorial pages to pulpits, editors and preachers railed against them. The budget for one of their balls or their summer wardrobe could feed hordes of starving poor. The examples set by this class came under constant attack.

This group through its lifestyle was accused of many sins, but, as we shall see, one of them was not dullness.

The Newport invasion was led by the pioneering August Belmonts. As a member of the Rothschild family, August Belmont Senior was gilded with European banking money, and his wife Caroline was the daughter of Commodore Matthew Perry. Their mansion, By-the-Sea, was one of the first along Bellevue Avenue.

The Belmonts began throwing lavish parties and parading up Bellevue Avenue in their French carriage.

The Old Guard was offended by such exhibitions, but their protests were futile as the floodgates opened before a rush of Astors, Vanderbilts, Van Rensselaers, and Stuyvesants. The Belmonts proved to be bellwethers.

Thus began the Gilded Age of Newport, the splendor of which the world has rarely seen. The summer colonists built their lavish mansions (always called cottages no matter what their size or cost) along Bellevue Avenue and around Ochre Point and Ocean Drive.

Newport became the Mecca for high society and a playground for the new American aristocrats.

Mrs. Stuyvesant Fish

OF MANSIONS AND MADNESS

So, the Gilded Agers made Newport their summer Mecca, and the race was on. Competition for position in the social order was intense. Even Old Line New York families like the Van Alens and the Goelets found themselves drawn into the fray as the struggle of upmanship expanded.

Of course financial strength and genealogy played a role in social standing, but as the Gilded Age developed, other factors rose to prominence. The size, grandeur, and location of one's cottage were critical, and other issues, such as lavish balls, expensive wardrobes, and fancy yachts, were important.

COTTAGES AND KINGS

The Cottagers chose Bellevue Avenue, Ochre Point, and Ocean Drive as the stage for their exhibitionism. Here they built a most magnificent and monumental collection of private residences. All sorts of architectural styles were represented, ranging from stately Victorian manor houses to Italian Renaissance villas to French chateaus to English castles.

Richard Morris Hunt and Stanford White were the premier architects of the Gilded Age. Although they both designed a series of stately and tasteful Newport cottages (particularly White), they also contributed greatly (particularly Hunt) to the collection of magnificent stone palaces that are so dominant. Architectural purists have called these creations absurd white elephants and condemned the designers for their corruption. Nevertheless, Hunt and White were prolific and powerful forces in the gilded culture.

Rosecliff, c. 1900

Stanford White of the New York architectural firm of McKim, Mead and White was the creator of Tessie Oelrich's Rosecliff, Mamie Fish's Crossways, Edwin Morgan's Beacon Rock, the famed Newport Casino, and several other elegant shingle-style cottages. However, it was Richard Morris Hunt who had the most profound impact on the architecture of the time.

Educated at the Beaux Arts school in Paris, where he embraced the "classic" style of architecture, Hunt translated his training to the United States and led the so-called American Renaissance revolution in architecture.

The timing was right, as Hunt's bent toward the classic European style of architecture matched with the unlimited wealth and the burning desire for ostentation of the Gilded Agers.

Hunt became the architect-in-residence for the Vanderbilts, the Belmonts, and the Goelets, and designed the most famous Newport mansions: The Breakers (Cornelius Vanderbilt), Marble House (William K. Vanderbilt), Belcourt Castle (O.H.P. Belmont), and Ochre Court (Ogden Goelet). He also designed no less than George Washington Vanderbilt's mind-boggling Biltmore estate in the North Carolina mountains and William K. Vanderbilt's imposing French chateau on Fifth Avenue.

THE SOCIAL GATEKEEPER

For two months each summer the social invasion was in full force. In its early stages, Newport society was shaped by one Ward McAllister, the developer of the famous list of four hundred. Mister Make-a-Lister, as he was called, asserted that there were only "about four hundred people in fashionable New York society. If you go outside that number you strike people who are either not at ease in a ballroom or make other people not at ease."

McAllister was a southern lawyer with roots in Newport as an early summer colonist. He bought a Newport farm and threw many popular picnics. McAllister was an expert at party planning, a master of pomposity, and snob *par excellence*. He filled a vacuum in a rapidly developing social world by becoming its aribter. He soon latched on to Mrs. Caroline Astor, a prime mover who made him the gatekeeper of society.

When McAllister died in 1895, he was succeeded by the even more bizarre and certainly more interesting Harry Lehr.

BALLS AND DINNERS

The balls and dinner parties of Newport society were unmatched and would surely rival those from any previous era.

The Pembroke Joneses from North Carolina earmarked $300,000 for entertaining during each Newport season. A single Newport ball could cost as much as $200,000. Mrs. Elbridge Gerry and Mrs. Ogden Mills claimed that they could throw a party for a hundred without adding to their servant staff.

This was Newport at its social apex; ten-course meals with solid gold services were par for the course.

At the infamous "Dogs Dinner," sponsored by Elizabeth Drexel Lehr and Mamie Fish, a hundred dogs feasted on stewed liver, rice, and fricassee of bones. It took the twisted mind of Harry Lehr to concoct such an unusual event that featured all manner of society's canines, some appropriately dressed for the occasion, dining on the veranda of the Lehr cottage. The "Dogs Dinner," occurring during the mid-1890s depression, gained national publicity and rebuke from the pulpits and editorial pages.

Costume balls were common in Newport, and they reached great heights of innovation.

At Mamie Fish's Mother Goose Ball in 1913, 200 guests were attired in costumes based on Mother Goose nursery rhymes, and her Crossways mansion was fully decked in Mother Goose motif.

Mrs. Stuart Duncan at the Mother Goose Ball, 1913

Henry Clews, Jr., the Wall Street brokerage heir, held a parodical Servants' Ball. Guests were invited to dress as the servant of their choice. It was a ball that didn't amuse the servant corps. Guests arrived to witness a Harry Lehr greeting as butler, Tessie Oelrichs mopping the floor, and O.H.P. Belmont taking cloaks.

One costume ball prompted a fitting malapropism from a bewildered footman when he announced a diminutive Henry Carter dressed as Henry IV and his rotund wife dressed as a Norman peasant. The confused footman's announcement was loud and clear: "Henry IV and an enormous pheasant."

Rosecliff was the setting for some of Newport's most memorable balls (and it still is). For the White Ball, Tessie Oelrich's elegant terra-cotta chateau was decked entirely in white, and guests wore nothing but white. Revelers could look out from the country's largest ballroom and view a veritable fleet of full-sized model ships, with their white sails billowing, decorating the back lawn.

The height of decadence, in the eyes of many, was the famous Monkey Dinner. In another creation from the contorted mind of Harry Lehr, and in collusion with Mamie Fish, a monkey in full formal dress was the surprise guest of honor at Lehr's mansion. Guests were invited to meet Price del Drago, a Corsican nobleman, but what they got was a tuxedoed monkey who behaved rather well during dinner, but took to the chandeliers and began throwing lightbulbs after the champagne caught up with him. It was all hilariously amusing for the guests, but a collective gasp could almost be heard from the Old Line Newporters, and of course the newspapers had a field day.

RULES AND RITUALS

In the early part of the Gilded Age, when Mrs. Astor was in firm control, it was much more difficult for wealthy upstarts to penetrate society's barriers. Mrs. Astor insisted that candidates for the exalted circle be cleansed of the effects of working in trade. It usually took two generations for the money to cool off. Later, these standards didn't hold up and were replaced by more subjective and political criteria.

But you didn't enter Newport society in one year, no matter who you were. If you were an aspiring social gate crasher, you'd be advised to move gradually. First you may want to spend a season in Bar Harbor, get to know some of the right people. Then if you go to Newport, don't buy a cottage, maybe just rent one. If you can, find a patron, a supporter from the upper echelons of the Four Hundred. Try to get invited to an important party. And if you do, don't try to out-dress, out-jewel, or out-entertain any of the established socialites. This would be the kiss of death. And remember, when you're out in your coach on Bellevue Avenue for an afternoon drive, don't ever overtake a woman of higher social standing.

Exchanging calling cards was an unusual ritual peculiar to Gilded Age society. Most summer afternoons, the family, dressed to the nines, boarded their shiny coach, driven by liveried coachmen decked in family colors (maroon for Vanderbilts and blue for Astors), to call on other women of equal caste. At this point, the men would try to repair to the Reading Room or their yacht.

Strangely, the visitors never entered their neighbor's cottage, but if they had, the mistress would have been out in her coach visiting other neighbors. Callers merely sent their footman in to leave a calling card with the neighbor's footman. This could consume a great part of the afternoon.

This puzzling ritual was extremely formal and often preceded a full-blown coaching parade along Bellevue Avenue and around Ocean Drive. Victorias, phaetons, four-in-hands, and all manner of shiny black coaches participated in the exhibition. Stiff-backed and poker-faced, the coachmen ritualistically drove the ten-mile route, while the matrons solemnly bowed to one another in cult-like recognition.

A stroll down Bellevue Avenue

The constraints on members of the privileged class could be smothering, particularly for the children. Girls were especially affected.

In Consuelo Vanderbilt's memoirs, she complains about her morning attire, which consisted of a floor-length dress with a high and tight whalebone collar and a corset strangling her waist to the prescribed eighteen inches. Her huge hat was festooned with flowers and feathers and held to her hair with long steel pins. A veil hid her face, and tight gloves squeezed her hands. All she needed was her parasol, and she

14

was off to Bailey's Beach for her morning dip!

Wearing her dark dress and black stockings, she bobbed in the waves, protected from the sun by her large hat.

Consuelo abhorred the daily tedium, which included no sports like tennis or golf but, instead, finishing-school type lessons in deportment and etiquette. She was constantly controlled and censored by her governess and her mother.

When marriage came, the control was highly evident, particularly in Consuelo's case. She was the victim of a bitter brokered marriage to the Duke of Marlborough, which eventually ended in divorce.

Consuelo Vanderbilt, the Duchess of Marlborough

MARRIAGE NEWPORT STYLE

In Newport, marriage brokering was extensive, and, not surprisingly, so was divorce. Many of the Vanderbilts and most of the Astors (particularly the later generations) were divorced. John Jacob Astor VI's marital affairs were so complicated that he petitioned the New York court to decide which woman was his wife, and Cornelius Vanderbilt IV was married seven times.

Automobile magnate William Budlong was sued for divorce twenty-one times. On several occasions, Mrs. Budlong exiled him from their mansion, and he was relegated to morning entreaties before her bedroom window in order to get a clean shirt. Eventually they were divorced for good.

Since many of these marriages were not founded on love, infidelity was not unusual. In Cornelius Vanderbilt IV's memoirs he describes his mother discussing this issue with his aunt, May Goelet, on the lawn of her mansion, Ochre Court. "Of course he has a mistress," was the nonchalant remark.

In her autobiography, Blanche Oelrichs describes illicit trysts in the woods near Hanging Rock overlooking Sachuest Beach.

BACKSTAIRS

The servant staff, obviously the backbone of mansion operations, was stratified into a highly structured caste system. Everyone knew his place in this social microcosm. The butler and chief chef were the highest rank, and personal maids and valets were much higher in status than footmen, stable boys, or upstairs maids. A butler would not serve dinner or empty ashtrays; he might not even answer the door. A woman's personal maid would not make a bed or clean the bedroom.

In addition to the butlers, chefs, maids, valets, stableboys, and footmen, there were coachmen, nannies, governesses, social secretaries, gardeners, and yacht crews. This group often performed herculean feats that were largely unrecognized. This often related to planning and executing enormously complex dinners, parties, or balls with little advance warning.

Azar, O.H.P. Belmont's Arabian valet, was a colorful character around Belcourt Castle. With his flashy military jacket and red fez, he attentively stood behind Belmont's enormous armchair as guests were greeted in the Grand Hall at Belcourt. After Belmont promoted him to chief butler, Azar would dazzle guests in uniforms glittering with gold. He exuded an overwhelming aura of grandeur and superiority, as he stood between two English footmen in full livery and powered hair, and greeted guests with ultimate pomp and circumstance.

Morton, Mamie Fish's butler, was the model of impassiveness. He awed even his employers with his haughtiness and unruffled superiority. After all, he had served English royalty. However, one day after a tiff with Mrs. Fish over an unusual number of luncheon guests, he was fired. In revenge, he disassembled all of her gold dinner service the night before a large dinner party at Crossways.

The servants generally got little respect and even less salary, but in those days there were plenty of them available — such that Perry Belmont would station a footman holding a candelabrum on every sixth step of the Belcourt Castle stairway.

Even well-known professional entertainers were treated as second class to the Four Hundred. When Mrs. Cornelius Vanderbilt engaged violinist Fritz Kreisler to play at one of her dinner parties, he quoted her a fee of thirteen thousand dollars. Without a blink she agreed, but then asked him not to mix with her guests after the performance. Then with a masterful rejoinder, Kreisler quickly responded, "In that case, my fee is only five hundred."

Bonniecrest, Mr. and Mrs. Stuart Duncan

THE GILDED PLAYGROUND

In the late 1800s, leisure time activities began to flourish. The prosperity at the dawn of the Gilded Age spawned several gentleman sports, and this was nowhere more evident than in Newport, where golf, tennis, polo, yachting, coaching, and automobiling were integral elements of an emerging society.

Of course, Newport became famous as the home of the America's Cup for more than fifty years. The Newport Country Club was the scene of the first American amateur golf championship. The Newport Casino hosted the first national tennis championship, in 1881, and is currently the home of the Tennis Hall of Fame. And so on.

The automobile was common in turn-of-the-century Newport. Resorters called them "bubbles," and considered them a novelty. Still, Newport is credited with promoting the automobile craze, for people all over wanted what Newport society had.

America's first automobile race was run on Sachuest Beach, as steamers, electrics, and internal combustion contraptions—manned by queer-looking drivers decked in dusters, goggles, long gauntlet gloves, and caps with huge visors—chugged, whirled, and jerked down the two-mile course at twenty miles per hour.

It never dawned on the cottagers that automobiles would be anything more than a passing fancy. Stuyvesant Fish would later recall, "Nobody dreamed that automobiles would come into general use."

On the other hand, the shiny black horse-drawn coaches were much more popular, and eleaborate coaching parades along Bellevue Avenue were highlights of a summer season.

The love affair with horses was extensive and highly developed. The horses lived the good life in enormous stone stables along Coggeshall Avenue, one block below Bellevue.

In the late 1800s, the rapidly emerging wealthy class was growing in power and wealth and in the process established various institutions of leisure to enhance its gaiety. Private clubs and societies of exclusivity appeared, one of the most notable being the Newport Casino, America's first country club.

THE CASINO AND THE COMMODORE

The Newport Casino was the brainchild of James Gordon Bennett, Jr., an overbearing iconoclast who was a publishing and yachting pioneer. Bennett was truly a driven man and created the Casino out of spite for the Newport establishment.

Bennett was the publisher of the *New York Herald* and the *Paris Herald*, and he was also famous for sending Stanley into Africa to find

Livingstone. He was a yachtsman extraordinaire and was a commodore of the New York Yacht Club. Bennett was a flamboyant big spender who easily went through thirty million dollars on his various whimsical projects.

The man could likely be reincarnated in today's Ted Turner, the famous broadcast magnate and America's Cup skipper who has paralleled Bennett's lifestyle and accomplishments in so many ways.

It seems that Bennett, an early Newport resorter, was in a rowdy mood one day when he challenged his friend, Captain "Sugar" Candy, a British lancer and polo player, to gallop his horse across the porch of the venerable Newport Reading Room. Candy accepted the challenge and charged up the stairs and into the hall, routing the astonished clubmen.

The Board of Governors of the Reading Room censured Bennett and withdrew Captain Candy's guest invitation. A relatively mild admonishment it was, but enough to enrage Bennett, who felt he had carte blanche in Newport.

Anyway, Bennett decided to supplant the stodgy Reading Room with a modern country club that would include lawn tennis courts, card rooms, a theater, and a restaurant. So, he hired the prominent architect Stanford White to create a most elegant complex.

Despite Bennett's imperious manner, he gave White a free hand in designing the Casino. The block-long complex was built on upper Bellevue Avenue.

The clubhouse combined Victorian charm with Chinese detail. Its shingled exterior and multi-gabled roof line surrounded a picturesque courtyard with a clock tower, horseshoe piazza, and several latticed

Newport Casino

19

porches. Mullaly's String Orchestra played on the piazza each morning, while club members gossiped from the second floor terrace.

The Casino opened in 1880, and in 1881, it hosted the first national tennis championship, the United States Lawn Tennis Tournament. The tournament remained at the Casino until 1915, when it moved to Forest Hills, New York (now it's called the U.S. Open and is at Flushing, New York).

In those days only bluebloods played in tournaments, and Boston Brahmin Richard Sears, decked in knickers, with wool socks, blazer, cap, and rubber-soled canvas shoes, won the championship eight years in a row.

Tennis Week was a social highlight every August as Newport's elite displayed themselves to each other in the highest of fashion. Grandstand seats were status symbols granted by birthright to the cream of American society. Of course, every year the same seats went to the Vanderbilts, the Astors, the Belmonts, and the Goelets.

With its social, theatrical, and athletic activities, the Casino became the cultural center of Newport. The tennis games, concerts, and dances were widely attended.

The Casino helped usher in a new era of social life. It was the Gay Nineties, formality and lavish entertainment were coming into vogue, and balls and banquets were replacing intimate dinners and high teas.

THE YACHTING CAPITAL OF THE WORLD

Pleasure yachting on a grand scale got its start in Newport. The early yachts of the Gilded Age were truly magnificent and costly.

Only the highest strata of society could afford such extravagant luxuries. The Vanderbilt yachts were legendary for their luxurious accommodations and sheer size. At 285 feet, William K. Vanderbilt's *Alva* was the largest and most expensive yacht of its time (1886). After *Alva* sank, Willie K. replaced her with the even larger *Valiant*, and later Cornelius Vanderbilt III, himself a commodore of the New York Yacht Club, built the steam yacht *North Star*, one of the largest of its time.

During this golden age of the private yacht, Newport harbor was the summer anchorage for such fabulous vessels as J.P. Morgan's *Corsair*, with its crew of eighty-five; James Gordon Bennett's steam yacht *Lysistrata*; the Astors' *Nourmahal*; the Drexels' *Sultana*; the Leeds' *Norma*; and the Wideners' *Josephine*. Mrs. Richard Cadwalader's 407-foot *Savarona* was too large for the harbor, and the world's largest yacht, sporting a full-sized pipe organ and decked with Persian rugs and tapestries, had to anchor out in Narragansett Bay.

Bennett's *Lysistrata* sailed the world and was equipped with a Turkish bath and a miniature dairy. The unpredictable Bennett once absconded with three prominent women (including a countess and a lady) during a dinner party for them aboard his yacht in Newport Harbor. After quaffing generous amounts of champagne, Bennett ordered the yacht to sea and promptly passed out in his cabin. When the ladies pleaded with the first officer to return to Newport, he simply stated that he had orders from the commodore to sail for Egypt. They had to wait until morning, when the commodore awoke and agreed to return home.

Although Newport hosted several important yacht races each summer, in 1930 the America's Cup series arrived (with its magnificent J-boats), and the City by the Sea was officially sanctified as the yachting captial of the world.

LIFE WAS A BEACH

As a beach, it was no big deal (Newport had several that were much better); nevertheless, Bailey's was the ultimate beach. Bailey's Beach was a postage stamp of sand and seaweed at the southern end of Bellevue Avenue. Modest in size, the Spouting Rock Beach Association (its formal name) was probably the most difficult (and therefore the most sought after) private club to join in all of American society.

A resorter might make it into the Casino, the Clambake Club, or even the Reading Room, but Bailey's Beach was always the toughest. Its exclusivity was even more pronounced because its facilities were so limited. There were only eighty-one outside cabanas.

Protocol was strictly enforced; no transgressions were permitted; bathers had to be covered from head to toe. Bathing at Bailey's was a full-dress affair.

Bailey's was far from luxurious; dressing rooms were simple wooden cubicles. Its cachet was its clientele. They were the creme de la creme, and membership was the greatest social merit badge.

Bailey's Beach, c. 1930

The Bailey's "bathing suit" was a far cry from today's bikini. Proper Newport society would be a laughing stock by modern standards. The women would be exceptionally hilarious in their standard-issue black regalia. Long black skirts over heavy black pantaloons and black stockings were common. Some even wore awkward black bathing shoes.

One day, tremors went up and down Bellevue Avenue when Mrs. Herbert Parsons dared to appear without the prescribed black stockings.

The men could be a bit eccentric, too. Herman Oelrichs would float for hours fully loaded with picnic pail, whiskey flask, cigar box, and a stack of books, and James Van Alen usually bathed with his monocle, straw hat, and cigar.

THE HORSEY SET

On the surface, it seemed mild enough: pedigreed horses pulling elegant black coaches in a parade along Bellevue Avenue.

But there was another side to the sport of coaching, and James Gordon Bennett, Jr., was its principal promoter. Bennett was a speed merchant; he loved to race and not just in organized races. He would fly down country roads driving at breakneck speeds, sometimes in the middle of the night. Often after a few drinks, he would take reckless midnight rides, driving naked in the coach box. "I want to be able to breathe," he explained.

In one incident, Bennett nearly affected the outcome of history when he went on a wild coaching ride with Jennie Jerome, the future mother of Winston Churchill. They were nearly killed when Bennett flipped the coach while careening around a corner.

Bennett and some of the so-called Belmont clique (Leonard Jerome, August Belmont, William Travers, and Henry Clews) introduced coaching to Newport.

In addition to coach racing, coaching parades were highly popular. An entire subculture and jargon developed around the sport. Form and dress were important ingredients. A "whip" was a coaching aficionado who observed proper protocol while driving. He would be decked in a vivid green topcoat and boutonniere, a yellow-striped waistcoat, silk top hat, and shiny patent-leather boots. A "whip" could become a "howling swell" by attaching a bunch of flowers to the neck of each horse.

This more serene side of coaching was really an exhibition of one's wealth and status. During the Gay Nineties, all manner of tiny phaetons, low victorias, elegant landaus, convertible barouches, and four-in-hands could be seen clattering along Bellevue Avenue, with tooting horns, cracking whips, and jingling chains. The equipment was fancy, and everything gleamed with polish and wax, from the coachmen's boots to the horses' hides.

The unique August Belmont coach was drawn by four horses, the lead

Mr. and Mrs. Alfred Vanderbilt after a coaching victory

two mounted by postillions dressed as jockeys.

The formal parade was a daily highlight along Bellevue Avenue, but the stiffness and aloofness of the participants would make it seem a bizarre ritual by today's standards.

The horses, the central figures of the show, were highly trained steeds. The high-stepping leaders were like seasoned actors haughtily tossing their heads, while the wheelers kept their hoofs low to the ground, anchoring the team.

August Belmont was considered a great reinsman, and his horses "Rockingham" and "Waltzingham" were classic high-steppers. Alfred Vanderbilt drove a great duo in "Schoolgirl" and "Lady Teazle." Reggie Vanderbilt's horses, hailing from Sandy Point farm, may have been the best in Newport; he won several prizes with his favorite horse "Doctor Schwonk." Pierre Lorillard's "Parole" won purses of $118,000, an astronomical sum at that time.

Horses were treated royally in their huge stone stables, their every need attended to by a retinue of stable hands. O.H.P. Belmont couldn't bear to be too far from his horses, so his were lodged on the first floor of Belcourt Castle. Richard Morris Hunt, the architect of the Breakers, designed their stalls. Belmont gave them changes of equipment three times a day and provided gold-embroidered white linen sheets for their bed.

Belmont loved his horses so much that he had his two favorites stuffed and mounted on the second floor of Belcourt.

Mrs. Alva Vanderbilt Belmont had two saddles, one for riding left, the other for riding right, which she alternated regularly to protect her figure from distortion.

The annual September horse show at the Casino was well attended by the barons of Newport, segregatged from the commoners in their exclusive hundred dollar boxes.

Elsie French Vanderbilt and E.J. Berwind at
Newport polo

MRS. ASTOR

The Queen of Newport

She was known simply as Mrs. Astor. But she was the mistress of Beechwood, Newport's first queen, and the high priestess of American society.

Caroline Schermerhorn Astor was the ruler of the Four Hundred and the trailblazer for an emerging aristocratic class. In collaboration with her prime minister, Ward McAllister, she built American society on a grand scale, established its rules and rituals, and decided who belonged and who didn't. Jews, Irish, and most Catholics were generally excluded.

The Mrs. Astor

In the early days, Mrs. Astor had near dictatorial powers over her class. People likened her to Queen Victoria; she dressed the part and acted the part.

Mrs. Astor was like a cult figure; everyone paid homage. The recognition she bestowed upon an aspiring social climber usually meant the difference between high society membership and social oblivion.

She raised jewel wearing to a high plateau of ostentation. She never wore jewelry during the day, but at night she became a dazzling spectacle in her trademark diamond tiara, a stunning diamond stomacher, a triple-stranded diamond necklace (204 stones), and various chains of diamonds dispersed about her person. Also, her fingers were covered with rings of diamonds and other precious stones.

According to Mrs. Astor's dictum, it took three generations of wealth untainted by work "in trade" to qualify for social acceptability. The money had to "cool off," as she put it. Conveniently, Mrs. Astor's husband was the grandson of *The* John Jacob Astor I, and the Astor fortune was invested in real estate, an acceptable pursuit. Not just money, but lineage was also essential for entree into the rarefied air of high society. Mrs. Astor's pedigree traced back to New York Dutch aristocracy of the Knickerbocker period.

However, the Vanderbilts, in spite of their millions, still worked in the railroads and, therefore, didn't exist in Mrs. Astor's world. Of course, this all changed when the formidable Alva Vanderbilt extorted Mrs. Astor's imprimatur when Alva agreed to invite her debutante daughter to an absolutely critical coming-out ball.

Physically, Mrs. Astor appeared an unlikely candidate for her exalted stature; she was far from beautiful and looked somewhat dumpy with her short stature, large jaw, and prominent nose.

Mrs. Astor's husband, William Backhouse Astor, Jr., was a rather dour gentleman who lacked the refinement and ambition to accompany his wife on her social adventures. William was much more concerned with horse breeding, yachting, and womanizing—not necessarily in that order. Parties aboard his sailing yacht, *Ambassadress*, or his steam yacht, *Nourmahal*, usually included a multitude of unescorted women; they never included Mrs. Astor.

William's grandfather, John Jacob Astor, the founder of the family fortune, was an illiterate German immigrant who came to America in 1784 with $25 in his pocket. He became interested in the fur business and rapidly rose from simple fur trader to monopolist over the American market. As his fur business expanded, he invested the profits in real estate, and by 1835 he was the richest man in the world.

Eventually, the Astor family real estate holdings became so extensive that the Astors were known as the landlords of New York City.

John Jacob left his son, William Backhouse Astor, an estate valued at $40 million. William doubled his inheritance and left $80 million to be divided between his two sons, John Jacob Astor III and William Backhouse Astor, Jr. (Mrs. Astor's husband).

With the Astor millions behind her, Mrs. Astor was heavily armed for her ascendancy. In the early 1870s, the Astor's Fifth Avenue mansion was the seat of social power, as Mrs. Astor began collaborating with Ward McAllister to set the standards and establish the caste system that would govern society.

Her annual New York ball was the pinnacle of each social season. An invitation was prized by every socialite, since it ratified her elite status. After dinner and before dancing, Mrs. Astor would hold court from a long couch (appropriately known as the throne), receiving visitors she personally selected for special attention. This practice identified her favorites for the upcoming social season.

In the late 1880s, Mrs. Astor set up summer court in Newport, when she opened her Bellevue Avenue cottage, Beechwood. The cottage, bordered on three sides by a spacious piazza, had been a Newport attraction for many years. Mrs. Astor added a ballroom, the largest in Newport at that time. The elegant and tasteful Beechwood was quite different from the overpowering marble palaces that were built later by the Vanderbilts.

The dinner parties at Beechwood were the epitome of Gay Nineties elegance. Guests were immersed in an overwhelming atmosphere of gold, crystal, and flowers. Blue-liveried footmen (copied from Windsor Castle) served dinner on gold plates; roses and candelabra abounded. Guests would feast on ten courses over three or four hours.

For a time, a bitter battle raged over ownership of the title "Mrs. Astor." It seems the William Waldorf Astors set up housekeeping at the charming Beaulieu mansion, next to Mrs. Astor at Beechwood. William Waldorf, the son of John Jacob Astor III and Mrs. Astor's nephew, insisted that his wife, the former Mary Dahlgren Paul, be addressed as *The* Mrs. Astor.

This caused some confusion at the Newport post office when letters for both women were addressed simply as "Mrs. Astor, Newport, Rhode Island." Eventually, with Ward McAllister's help, Caroline won the title on the basis of seniority and personality strength.

In any case, the Waldorf Astors soon moved to London, where they established the famous English branch of the family.

The English Astors included the famous Lady Astor, the daughter-in-law of William Waldorf. Lady Astor, the former Nancy Langhorne, held a seat in the House of Commons for 25 years and was known as a flamboyant and witty campaigner. In one typical incident, while speaking in a farming district, she encountered a remark from a sarcastic farmer, who said, "Say, missus, how many toes are there on a pig's foot?" She came back with the rejoinder, "Take off your boots man and count for yourself."

The American Astors were sometimes called the decadent Astors, while the English were known as the artistocratic Astors.

The marriage of Mrs. Astor's eldest daughter, Emily, to James Van Alen nearly resulted in a duel when her father insulted the Van Alens by insinuating that they were unworthy to marry Astors. William Astor later apologized.

Another daughter, Charlotte, married James Drayton of Philadelphia and later had a lurid and widely reported love affair with Hallett Alsop Borrowe, a vice-president of Equitable Life. In a gesture of hypocrisy, her playboy father disinherited her.

Mrs. Astor's son, John Jacob Astor IV, married Philadelphia socialite and outstanding beauty Ava Willing. He was an army colonel and fought in the Spanish-American War. In 1910, 46-year-old Colonel Jack Astor stunned society by divorcing Ava and marrying an 18-year-old girl, Madeleine Force.

The newlyweds soon left for Europe, to wait until the incident blew over. When they returned in 1912, they sailed on the ill-fated cruise ship *Titanic*. Astor went down with the ship, but his wife, pregnant with John Jacob Astor VI, was saved. Astor left an $87 million estate, $63 million of it in real estate.

In her later years, a disillusioned Mrs. Astor quietly withdrew from the front lines of society. She threw her last great ball in 1905, before going permanently into seclusion. Caroline Schermerhorn Astor, the queen of Newport, spent her last years as a senile recluse in Beechwood mansion.

Ava Willing Astor before divorce

John Jacob Astor IV with wife Madeleine, 1911

KING LEHR

The Story of Harry and Bessie

The story of Harry and Bessie matches one of the most bizarre characters of the Gilded Age with a fabulously wealthy heiress caught in a web of unhappiness. To a large extent, Elizabeth Drexel was a perfect fit for Harry Lehr's neurotically warped personality. She was naive, lonely, and above all, rigidly scrupulous.

Harry and Bessie on their wedding trip, 1901

Harry Lehr, the son of a middle-class Baltimore tobacco merchant, rose to become the court jester of Newport society. He was so entertaining at balls and got along so well with the matrons of society — none other than Alva, Tessie, Mamie, and Mrs. Astor were his principal supporters — that he became entrenched as a social trendsetter. Although his meteoric career was initially self-made through intense and persistent honing of his skills as a doting bon vivant, it was Elizabeth (Bessie) who financed its continuation.

Harry intitially established himself in Baltimore society as an agreeable and affable Gilded Age groupie. He gradually gathered attention as a party entertainer and was constantly in demand to play the piano, tell jokes, dance, speak French, or discourse on fashion or party planning.

His big break came when Mrs. Evelyn Townsend Burden invited him to Fairlawn, her Newport cottage. It was the beginning of Newport's lushest era, fertile ground for Harry's career development. Mrs. Astor soon recognized Harry's social skills, and with her sponsorship his career flourished rapidly.

Under Mrs. Astor's tutelage, Harry's first Newport season was a great success. With his gift of showmanship and irresistible laugh, Harry became a prized decoration at dinner parties and balls.

Harry was by no means a lazy layabout. As a professional sycophant and master student of high society, he ambitiously and eagerly honed his skills.

His first winter season in New York was triumphant as he dined regularly at Sherry's with Mrs. Astor and was intensely tracked by the society pages. Harry gradually evolved from a social participant to a leader and trendsetter.

Bessie at Court Ball, Dresden

Still virtually penniless, Harry managed to live the high life through his connections to the dowagers and matrons of New York society. His network of endorsements would be the envy of any modern-day professional athlete. The managements of Delmonico's and Sherry's were more than happy to have Harry dine gratis. He never paid at the Waldorf-Astoria; his imprimatur was enough. Jewelers loaned him their jewels, and tailors tailored for him at no charge. He was even on the payroll of a French champagne company. When in Newport, he was an established guest shuttling between mansions.

Harry's repertoire included considerable gall and impudence. This counterbalanced his fawning and doting. He developed this skill to such an extent that his insults became sought-after status symbols. When Mamie Fish and her husband were leaving a party early, he shot at them, "Sit down Fishes, you're not rich enough to leave first."

Always debonair and natty, Harry was blue-eyed and blond with an alto voice and a trademark laugh. The men of Newport society had little use for the likes of Harry Lehr and his effete manner and love of women's fashions. They viewed him as the cause of more expenses as he helped their wives plan balls, try on gowns, and buy jewels.

Harry had no intention of relying on the munificence of Main Line society for long-term support. He needed a rich wife, but also one acceptable to society. Harry met Elizabeth Drexel Dahlgren through a mutual friend, Edith Gould. Elizabeth (Bessie), of the Maine Line Philadelphia Drexels, was a recently widowed heiress, and in her autobiography *King Lehr and the Gilded Age*, she describes the meeting at Mrs. Gould's opera party: "Suddenly the lights went up and Edith Gould turned to me. . . .

'"My dear, I want you to meet the most amusing man in New York. . . .'

"I looked up into eyes of vivid blue that seemed to hold the very spirit of gaiety. . . . He sat down at my side and we began to talk. In five minutes I had decided that Edith Gould was right; he was certainly the most amusing man that I had ever met. Conversation rippled around him. Impossible for anyone to be bored in his company."

Bessie was enamored of his charm and graciousness and rapidly fell in love. Harry had decided to marry Bessie but first invited her to lunch at Sherry's to meet the most powerful members of society at that time: Mrs. Astor, Tessie Oelrichs, Mamie Fish, and Alva Vanderbilt Belmont. Bessie must pass muster with this oligarchy, or Harry wouldn't consider marriage. Well, she did pass and describes the scene in her book. "As we rose to leave the restaurant I heard Mrs. Oelrichs say, 'I think she is delightful, Harry. We four are going to take her up. We will make her the fashion. You need have no fear. . . .'"

On the way home, Harry proposed.

Bessie intensely considered continuation of her "desperately lonely" life the way it was or starting a new life with Harry. She reflected on how her love for him was neither emotional nor passionate. She viewed it on a higher plane, one of respect, friendship, and affection. This perspective may have been the basis for her undoing.

She described their wedding ceremony with a sense of foreboding, and noted the absence of gaiety from Harry's vivid blue eyes; she only saw mockery.

On their wedding night, the future of the relationship was brought home to Bessie with stunning clarity. She planned a memorable evening at the Stafford Hotel in Baltimore.

"It was our wedding evening and I lingered over my dressing for this our first dinner alone, pinned a diamond brooch into my rose brocade gown, hoped that Harry would think me beautiful. In the adjoining dining room of our suite the table was being laid—the sheaves of crimson roses I had ordered filled the room with their fragrance. Caviar, quails in aspic, his favourite brand of champagne, the cabinet of cigars I had bought for him; I had forgotten nothing. By the side of his plate lay the gold and enamel watch I had chosen so carefully. I wanted us both to remember this evening all our lives."

Soon the maid came in with a message that Harry was dining alone, and that she should do likewise. Later, Harry appeared and told her the revolting truth.

He told Bessie that they would portray the happy couple in public, but in private he wanted nothing to do with her. He didn't love her, and he could never love her.

An overwhelmed Bessie could hardly whisper in response. "But why did you marry me?"

Harry, with his voice full of bitterness, told her the unvarnished truth—for her money, of course.

As Bessie was reeling with shock, Harry ended his sadistic speech by saying that they could get along quite well if she didn't come near him except in public, for, in fact, she repulsed him.

On the surface, Harry and Bessie were the loving couple, but underneath the thin facade there was a black hole.

Throughout their marriage, Bessie was the unfortuante subject of Harry's constant ridicule and belittlement. Harry had no use for his wife, either as a companion or a mate; she was merely a tool to use to further his social career. Harry must have known that Bessie would endure her loveless fate, for she could not bring herself to divorce. Her staunch old-school Catholic mother would not brook divorce, and she feared hurting her deeply.

Even years later, when Bessie fell in love with a shadowy man whose identity was never disclosed, she would not give up Harry. She called this man Mister X in her autobiography. In sad irony, after her mother died and Bessie resolved to cast Harry away, she received the news that Mister X had died.

Harry loved women's things and gloried in their fashions, jewels, and parties. Although his sexual orientation was never clearly defined, he showed no romantic interest in the opposite sex.

Harry Lehr was the pivot of the festive set of society, and, therefore, Bessie had to entertain lavishly, giving huge dinner parties. Harry aggressively pursued his vocation as social arbiter and mansion jester. He collaborated with the Great Triumvirate to make and shape social policy. In their view, the stodgy and staid aristocracy of the early Gilded Age needed to be transformed into a more cosmopolitan, hedonistic, and iconoclastic ruling class.

In her book, Bessie describes Newport as a social Mecca. It was the pinnacle of social acceptance, and Harry Lehr was its self-proclaimed guru. He readily dispensed advice on how to enter Newport society. Bessie paints a vivid picture of exclusivity: "Every summer Harry Lehr and I went to Newport like everyone else in our world, for in those days so much prestige was attached to spending July and August at the most exclusive resort in America that to have neglected to do so would have exposed a definite gap in one's social armour." Anyone who had an established position in society went to Newport; there simply was no other way, "for Newport was the very Holy of Holies, the playground of the great ones of the earth from which all intruders were ruthlessly excluded by a set of cast-iron rules." Those who stayed away did so because they were afraid.

Harry Lehr stated it succinctly: "Avoid Newport like the plague until you are certain that you will be acceptable there. If you don't, it will be your Waterloo." Many a wealthy social climber tried to penetrate Newport outside the established system, only to flee in abject humiliation.

Under Harry Lehr's tutelage, the morals of Newport society loosened. Many society women took weekday lovers, while their husbands labored on Wall Street. The men often commuted to Newport on the Fall River steamships on Friday nights and spent most of their weekends at the Reading Room or the Casino, or maybe retiring to their yacht in Newport harbor for a private party.

The parties and balls became much more lavish, and the conspicuous consumption led to disgust and cries of decadence from the general public. These excesses continued through the early part of the century, until the disruptions and fall-out from World War I put a serious crimp on lifestyles of such a grand scale.

Harry and Bessie traveled extensively in Europe and eventually bought a townhouse in Paris, and after World War I, they lived there most of the time. Harry eventually developed a brain disorder and died, mercifully bringing their twenty-eight year marriage to a close.

Bessie stayed in Paris, married an English baron, and became a prominent social leader.

THE GREAT TRIUMVIRATE

Alva, Mamie, and Tessie

The Great Triumvirate (Alva Belmont, Mamie Fish, and Tessie Oelrichs) consisted of three of the five most powerful women to rule Newport society throughout the Gilded Age, the other two being Mrs. Astor and Grace Wilson Vanderbilt.

A powerful trio—the driven Alva, the headstrong Tessie, and the abrasive Mamie collaborated to transform Newport society from the staid conservatism of Mrs. Astor to a more permissive and hedonistic institution. The three were unique in so many ways, but all possessed the unusual quality of spirited intelligence, a rare commodity among their peers.

Possibly the most influential and powerful woman of her time, **Alva Smith Vanderbilt Belmont** was the most durable member of the great Newport Triumvirate.

Alva dominated Newport society not through beauty or charm, but sheer willpower and boldness. Alva, an Alabama plantation belle, succeeded in marrying into two of the most powerful families of the Gilded Age. After gaining a sophisticated education at a French boarding school, she became a member of the southern aristocracy. In 1875, she visited the spa at White Sulfur Springs and met William K. Vanderbilt, the grandson of the famous Commodore. Then she accomplished what many post Civil War southern debutantes dreamed of: she married a Yankee millionaire.

It was Alva who succeeded in establishing the Vanderbilt name in the rarefied air at the social pinnacle. To do this, it was necessary to receive social recognition from Mrs. Caroline Astor, society's self-appointed Grand Dame. Initially, Mrs. Astor refused to acknowledge the social existence of the Vanderbilts, feeling threatened by their immense power and wealth. But Alva's gamesmanship was formidable. In 1883, Alva planned a spring ball at her Fifth Avenue mansion for the leading New York debutantes. Conveniently, Carrie Astor was just out of finishing school and ready to emerge into society. Carrie was crushed when no invitation was forthcoming; she was the only debutante excluded. Alva let it be known that since Mrs. Astor had never called at the Vanderbilt mansion, an invitation was impossible. Mrs. Astor finally capitulated and rode over to the Vanderbilt mansion. She stayed in her carriage as her footman delivered her calling card. That was all that was necessary, Carrie received her invitation, and the Vanderbilts received the ultimate social recognition.

By the early 1890s, Alva firmly established hegemony in Newport. She collaborated with the preeminent architect of his time, Richard Morris Hunt, to build an eleven-million-dollar marble mansion. Marble House opened in 1892 and secured for Newport the leadership of the

Alva

American Renaissance in classical architecture.

Alva was an imperious perfectionist and a heavy-handed tyrant. She never shied from educating her contemporaries on how to live and how to think. Even on a visit to Blair Castle in Scotland she criticized its authenticity.

In 1895, a battle royal erupted when daughter Consuelo balked at an arranged marriage to the Duke of Marlborough. Consuelo eventually relented and became one of several ill-fated American heiresses to marry a European title. In this fatally-flawed process, the American nouveau riche gained legitimacy for their status, and the European aristocrats gained immense financial power. Normally these were the only reasons. The usual result was a broken and bitter relationship, with the American woman getting short shrift in the form of abandonment, humiliation, and de facto robbery. This arrangement did little to help the United States balance of trade, since more than $200 million of inherited capital was swept across the ocean.

A dowry of $10 million accompanied Consuelo to Blenheim Castle, the ducal residence of Charles Richard John Spencer-Churchill, the ninth Duke of Marlborough. Entrance into the Churchill family was a costly venture, as millionaire Leonard Jerome could certainly have attested. Lord Randolph Churchill married his daughter Jennie (the mother of the great Winston) and significantly drained his sizable fortune in the process.

Both Consuelo and the Duke had hoped to marry their true loves. But these hopes were dashed in the face of duty and coercion.

Consuelo was not suited to the lifestyle of an English country duchess, and the daily tedium of her station gradually gave way to boredom. After eleven dismal years as mistress of the castle, she separated from the Duke, and they were eventually divorced.

At the same time Alva was negotiating with the hard-bargaining Churchills, her own marriage was unravelling rapidly. She and William K. were wholly incompatible. Her haughtiness contrasted considerably with his mild-mannered, relaxed, and unassuming demeanor. Devoted mostly to business and leisure, he rarely interfered in her management of the household.

After considerable domestic hostilities, including a series of intense and vituperative disputes aboard the Vanderbilt yacht on a cruise to India, they separated.

Even before the separation, William K. began spending more time on his yacht and with the Gilded Age equivalent of the international "Jet Set." He was rumored to be chasing women and neglecting the affairs of New York Central Railroad, the flagship of the Vanderbilt empire.

In 1895, Alva shocked her contemporaries and became the first leading socialite to divorce her husband. Then, in 1896, she stunned them again by marrying family friend Oliver Hazard Perry Belmont (reputed to be William K.'s best friend).

From that point on, Alva was ostrasized by the rest of the Vanderbilts, but not by the rest of society; she was too entrenched and ruthless for anyone to dare mount a successful coup. During the next summer in Newport, Alva resumed her dominant role as a member of the Great Triumvirate. She closed Marble House and moved across the street (Bellevue Avenue) to govern Belcourt Castle.

Alva dominated Perry Belmont much as she had William K., but their marriage remained intact until Belmont died in 1908.

Later, she embraced the women's suffrage movement, casting her enormous influence and wealth into the effort. Alva decried the exploitation of her sex and eventually recanted the attitudes that forced her daughter into an unwanted marriage. As a result, Consuelo was granted an annulment.

After Belmont's death, Alva reopened Marble House, and in 1913, she held a large garden party and rally in support of the suffrage movement.

After the summer of 1916, Alva never reopened Marble House and left Newport for good. She spent her last years in France, relentlessly promoting women's rights. She died in 1932.

Mrs. Herman Oelrichs possessed probably the most mundane heritage on Bellevue Avenue. Yet, she came to dominate Newport Society as a full-fledged member of the Great Triumvirate and mistress of the elegant mansion, Rosecliff.

Mrs. Oelrichs was the former Theresa Fair and was known as Tessie. Her childhood was nothing if not humble. Born in a California mining camp, Tessie was the daughter of James Fair, a lowly Irish immigrant who fled the devastating potato famine with his parents in 1843.

But for her father's extraordinary luck and tenacity, Tessie would likely have been just another frontier brat, shuttled from one squalid mining camp to another.

Fair was a canny and calculating swashbuckler who came to the

California goldfields by wagon train in 1849 and then proceeded to bide time building technical expertise in mining management. Fair focused his efforts not on placer mining (the washing of valuable minerals from sand deposits), but instead he searched for veins of gold-bearing quartz.

While working as a superintendent of a quartz mill in Angels Camp, California, he met Theresa Rooney, a pretty and winsome young widow. They married and had four children: Tessie, Virginia (known as Birdie), Charles, and James.

Around 1860, Fair made his move and joined the rush to the Nevada silver mines. Several years later in Virginia City, he formed a partnership with three other astute Irishmen, and they bought large tracts of mining claims.

Tessie

Up to this time, San Francisco bankers controlled Nevada mining development, but Fair and his associates bought up their holdings and transferred them to the group's newly-organized Bank of Nevada. They began vigorously digging shafts and tunnels, and in their Consolidated Virginia Mine they stumbled upon a pocket of gold and silver that may have been the most valuable single ore pocket ever found. It was Fair's dogged pursuit of a meager, meandering vein that led to the discovery of this astonishing bonanza.

The yield from the Consolidated Virginia Mine was so vast that it shook the market for gold and silver. The four partners went on to control the silver mining industry, and their take from the Comstock Lode amounted to more than $100 million. Fair parlayed his share into real estate, railroads, and other enterprises, and his eventual wealth was estimated at around $50 million.

Immense power and wealth unleashed the dark side of James Fair, and he became an accomplished practitioner of avarice, corruption, and blatant debauchery. He cheated in business, ran a successful but corrupt campaign for the U.S. Senate, and was an extensive womanizer. He had little use for the Senate and rarely participated in its functions.

Claiming adultery, his wife sued for divorce in 1883. The divorce settlement granted Mrs. Fair one-third of the estate and custody of Tessie and Birdie. Fair was charged with the care of Charles and James.

Theresa took Tessie and Birdie away to a life of refinement and private tutors. It seems the female Fairs were cut from a different bolt than the males. Fair had little interest in fatherhood and exercised limited control over the boys.

Son James nearly drank himself to death and eventually committed suicide. Charles was also a heavy drinker. He married against his father's will and was nearly disinherited. In 1902, Charles and his wife were killed in a high-speed auto accident near Paris.

The sisters decided to pursue a more discreet and genteel lifestyle, one of social position and brokered marriages. But Tessie was determined to broker her own marriage, and after sifting through a crop of fortune hunters, layabouts, and no-accounts, she settled on Herman Oelrichs, the son of a wealthy German shipping magnate. The Oelrichs family owned the North German Lloyd line of transatlantic ocean liners.

The spectacular San Francisco wedding (in 1890) was a magnificent social display attended by a large number of aristocrats and luminaries of the day. James Fair was not invited.

Herman's amiable personality contrasted sharply with the fiesty and headstrong Tessie. Although he was ten years her senior, the marriage made great social sense.

Tessie's mother died in 1891 (the same year the sisters purchased Rosecliff), and James Fair died in 1894 after living his last years alone in the Lick House, San Francisco. As a result, the sisters' net worth increased substantially. However, Fair left several wills, and his lecherous lifestyle produced a host of claimants to his fortune. For seven years, an incessant series of court battles depleted the estate and consumed much of Tessie's attention before all matters were finally settled.

After the wedding, Tessie's social sights were set on New York and Newport, and although Herman loved San Francisco, he deferred to her desires, and they moved East.

If Tessie's marriage was a sensible social alliance, then Birdie's was a brilliant social coup. In 1899, Tessie negotiated a match between her younger sister and William K. Vanderbilt II, the son of Alva and William K. Vanderbilt and great grandson of the famous Commodore.

Birdie may have been Tessie's alter ego. Tiny and mild-mannered, she contrasted sharply with the headstrong and regal Tessie. An 1894 picture at Bailey's Beach shows Birdie soaking wet and decked in a neck-to-ankle black "bathing suit" dress, with a big hat extending over her slightly pug nose. She cut a comical sight by today's standards, but she was right on the mark for the Gilded Age.

The society pages reported Birdie's wedding extensively. Just like Tessie's wedding, all the minutia was covered. The elite of New York society attended the reception at the Oelrich's Fifth Avenue mansion.

Vanderbilt gave his new wife a $75,000 pearl necklace.

They were light years from the dusty streets of Angel's Camp.

With time, Tessie and Herman gradually drifted apart. The romantic mismatch so common to socially-contracted marriages became apparent, and they began to live as far apart as they felt. He lived casually in his beloved San Francisco mansion, while she lorded over Rosecliff.

Tessie compensated for this marital vacuum by a single-minded devotion to her role as a baron of Newport society. She pretended intimacy with her husband and never publicly acknowledged the rift. Despite their geographic separation of continental proportions, she maintained the facade.

Tessie also feigned satisfaction with her powerful career on the Great Triumvirate. Blanche Oelrichs (Tessie's niece), in her autobiography, describes her aunt as seemingly restless, unhappy, and unfulfilled.

Tessie had the energy of a dervish and was completely immersed in her role. She ruled Rosecliff with drill instructor mentality, the mansion had to be spit-shined every day, and woe to the servant who was not equal to her standards. Her wrathful tongue scourged many an ear.

She masked her melancholy effectively as she dashed around Newport in her electric auto or whisked into the Casino flashing her classic Irish beauty and regal grace in huge hats with lace dresses adorning her hour-glass figure.

No doubt, like many intelligent and capable women of the time, she felt unfulfilled in her role and stifled in a society with norms so restrictive on female behavior and vocations. She turned to social and domestic pursuits as outlets for her boundless energy and found they came up short. They simply weren't enough.

However, Tessie had the added advantages bestowed by immense wealth and was therefore able to stamp an indelible imprint on history.

After Herman survived the 1906 earthquake, Tessie was so overwhelmed with relief that she vowed to repair their relationship. These efforts were dashed, however, when Herman returned to New York but visited his Fifth Avenue club before seeing his repentent wife. Tessie, after redecorating his room, buying him a new wardrobe, and laying out a romantic supper, was enraged and resumed the status quo.

Tessie and Herman never reconciled, and he died of a heart attack aboard a North German Lloyd liner. But there was one final bitter pill for Tessie.

Herman had left his meager half-million-dollar estate to his relatively unprosperous brother Charles. He wrongly assumed that Tessie would be satisfied with her millions. She contested the will and won half the estate.

Like so many others of her genre, Tessie spent her final days in a senile fantasy land, reliving old dinner parties and replaying the social highlights of days past.

Mrs. Stuyvesant (Mamie) Fish, the third member of the Great Triumvirate, was surely the most colorful of Newport hostesses. Mamie was a master satirist and an iconoclast with a great sense of humor. She had little use for the trappings of her class. She always seemed bored by her milieu, and yet she threw the most innovative and enjoyable parties. She insulted nearly everyone and was a gifted purveyor of one-liners.

Mamie hailed from Crossways, a magnificent Ocean Drive mansion with a commanding view of the pounding sea. Crossways has an overscaled Colonial portico supported by four Corinthian columns, but, consistent with the Fishes' relatively modest net worth, it doesn't exhibit the spectacle or monumentality of its exotic Bellevue Avenue cousins. Mamie would insist, "We're not rich, we have only a few million."

Mamie (born Mary Ann) had only a rudimentary education and could barely read or write. She was far from beautiful, save her sharp deep-black eyes. But she was the most sought after hostess in Newport.

Even though she was hardly educated, Mamie still seemed better suited to a more rewarding and meaningful life than that of a Gilded Age hostess.

Mamie married Stuyvesant Fish, her childhood sweetheart and possibly the most tolerant baron Newport has ever seen. Unlike many others, their marriage endured because they truly loved and understood each other. Stuyvesant was a professional manager and became president of the Illinois Central Railroad in 1887. Mr. Fish had no interest in society or ostentation, but when dealing with his wife, he was a paradigm of patience, with his unruffled manner and unpretentious attitude.

Mamie's tumultuous public life belied an extremely happy private life; in sharp contrast to her peers, she was a devoted wife and mother.

She was determined to attain social prominence by following an unorthodox path, and when she teamed up with the convoluted Harry Lehr (which she often did), the results were unpredictable. To Mamie, boredom was the ultimate sin.

Mamie worshipped no scared cows; she refused to participate in the social whirl of teas, card-calling, and ritualistic drives along Bellevue Avenue; she detested operas and musicales and would usually chatter endlessly throughout the program, much to the chagrin of the other guests. She got into a big row with James Van Alen when, knowing her incorrigible behavior, he invited only Mr. Fish and Mrs. Lehr (excluding Mamie and Harry Lehr) to a musicale. After she confronted Van Alen at Bailey's Beach and threatened to sabotage the affair, he relented but insisted that Mamie and Harry be exiled to the terrace while the music played.

Mamie had this disarming way of calling everyone "Sweet pet" or "Lamb," mainly because she was notorious for remembering names, but it also suited her mountainous indifference.

She would always welcome guests to her balls with an impatient "Howdy do, howdy do," moving them along with obvious annoyance.

Her sharp tongue could cut ice, and her barbs were thrown with deadly accuracy.

She once gave a luncheon for 50 ladies and refused to attend. She sat upstairs at Crossways and wouldn't come down despite the entreaties of her maid. "But Mrs. Fish, you invited them two weeks ago," the maid pleaded. Mamie dismissed her with a wave, "Tell them I've changed my mind."

Her one-liners were classic. "Make yourselves at home," she would tell her guests. "And believe me, there is no one who wishes you were there more than I do."

Once while her orchestra was playing "Home, Sweet Home," a male friend begged Mamie for one more two-step. She replied, "There are just two steps more for you, one upstairs to get your coat and the other out to your carriage."

Mamie

Even Harry Lehr, who had married the wealthy Elizabeth Drexel Dahlgren, was not safe. When he asserted that Mamie's favorite flower must be the climbing rose, she retorted, "And I know yours, pet. The Marigold."

Mamie even told Alva Belmont she looked like a toad.

The balls and dinners at Crossways were renowned; the miniscule staff (15 servants) and modest budget managed to produce Newport's most entertaining affairs.

Mamie's quest was to dominate and enliven society, and in the process she set new standards for entertaining. Breaking the mold of staid cotillions, she opened Crossways to all manner of lively entertainment. Dinner guests were treated to fetes ranging from a Marie Dresser comedy skit to the chorus line from *The Merry Widow* to an exhibition of John L. Sullivan's muscles. She even allowed celebrities to dine in the rarefied company of society's elite—a radical practice at the time.

Eschewing the lumbering three-hour dinners of other hostesses, Mamie regularly served eight-courses in less than an hour (her record was 30 minutes). Then it was on to the special entertainment.

Harry Lehr was Mamie's confidant and collaborator. On several occasions, they teamed up to surprise and amuse Newport society. They created the hilarious "Monkey Dinner" and the bizarre "Dogs' Dinner." They even fooled all of Newport society when Harry Lehr impersonated the Czar of Russia.

On this occasion, Mamie had planned to invite Grand Duke Boris of Russia, a house guest at Mrs. Ogden Goelet's Ochre Court, but her plans were scuttled when the two women feuded. To avoid a major embarrassment (her invitations were already sent), Harry Lehr appeared at Crossways disguised in medals and robes and entered with a flourish amidst bows and curtsies. Speaking in broken English, he reviewed an astounded but laughing line of guests.

Crossways

No one was immune to Mamie's abrasive tongue. It even led to the sacking of her husband after nearly 20 years as president of the Illinois Central, when E.H. Harriman, a formidable railroad baron, revengefully orchestrated a coup against Fish at an Illinois Central board meeting. The meeting erupted into a heated argument and ended with the decking of a board member by the fist of an enraged Stuyvesant Fish. Mr. Fish was out of a job and blackballed from the railroads.

The cause? Mamie again.

Mamie found Harriman's wife, Mary, unacceptable for social recognition (too dull), so she snubbed her from a Crossways tea party. After Harriman learned of this and of other insults at the party, he swore revenge, and Stuyvesant was his target.

Even though she invited them to fabulous and meticulously planned parties, Mamie seemed to repudiate her guests and always viewed them as a burden. It was the paradox of Mamie Fish: She recognized the triviality and senselessness of Gilded Age society, yet she aggressively sought its limelight.

To the end, Mamie was undaunted, relentless, and unswerving, and she still maintained her dominant social position in spite of her splendidly arrogant attitude—maybe because of it.

Mamie died of a stroke in 1915, just before her annual June 8 birthday party.

THE VANDERBILTS
Newport's First Family

The Vanderbilts are certainly the Gilded Age family most closely associated with Newport. Family members were intimately intertwined in Newport life. They owned two of the most prestigious mansions (The Breakers and Marble House), several lesser "cottages," and two large farms (Oakland and Sandy Point). Their matrons (Alva Vanderbilt Belmont, Alice Gwynne Vanderbilt, and Grace Wilson Vanderbilt) dominated Newport society, and their men were heavily involved in social clubs, charities, and leisure activities.

Cornelius Vanderbilt, Senior (1794–1877) established the family fortune, and when he died in 1877, he was the richest man in America. The legendary Cornelius Senior (known as the Commodore) was uncouth, shrewd, and driven. He was a visionary and an empire builder. The Commodore parlayed a humble Staten Island pole-powered ferryboat into a steamboat conglomerate transporting passengers and freight all along the Atlantic and Pacific coasts.

The trail-blazing Commodore established a lucrative New York-to-San Francisco transportation service. This innovative route traversed Nicaragua in an adventure-packed journey through river rapids and mountain jungles. The Commodore had found a way to shorten the trip to California and drew lucrative gold-rush traffic away from competitors who still used the isthmus of Panama. He even developed plans to build the first Central American canal, but these met stiff political opposition and never came to fruition.

However, shipping was only the beginning as the Commodore vastly expanded his fortune and power through railroads. Vanderbilt began buying railroads in the early 1860s when their economic importance was increasing rapidly. The Commodore built railroads, acquired railroads, consolidated railroads, and bribed legislators for rights of way and special preferences related to railroads. He established the New York Central, with its routes to the Great Lakes and vital link to the West, as the flagship of the Vanderbilt empire.

The Commodore was big and strong. His curly hair and busy sideburns framed a handsome face etched with distinction. He loved good cigars, but drank little alcohol, considering the practice a waste of time. He had scant education and a large storehouse of profanities which he used profusely.

Throughout his life, Vanderbilt attracted many enemies who were as ruthless as he, but few were as shrewd or as brassy. In confrontations, the Commodore usually came out on top and sometimes in spectacular fashion.

On several occasions, he bested his archenemy, an unscrupulous manipulator named Daniel Drew. But one particular confrontation proved enormously beneficial to the Commodore.

No altar boy himself, the Commodore had paid off an extremely corrupt New York legislature to approve consolidation of two of his railroads, the Hudson River and the Harlem. This move would reduce operating expenses and greatly benefit Vanderbilt.

However, Daniel Drew persuaded the New York legislators to doublecross Vanderbilt into believing he would get his way. The conspirators knew the price of Harlem stock would rise sharply on wind of the consolidation, so they planned to sell the stock short at the high price. Since a short sale is a promise to deliver a stock at the agreed price at some future date, they planned to buy the stock later at a much depressed price (after they voted against Vanderbilt's bill) and cover their short sales. In this way, they could buy low having already sold very high.

As expected, the price rose to 150, and Drew and the legislators sold short. Then the legislators voted against the consolidation and watched the stock price quickly plunge to 90. The legislators and Drew waited to buy at an even lower price, but the Commodore, his back against the wall, began a buying binge of Harlem stock. He mortgaged and sold properties in a desperate attempt to raise cash. Soon he and his brokers had bought all the shares, and there were none available for the short sellers to buy in order to make good on their promise. Vanderbilt controlled them all!

The conspirators would have to buy from him; there was no other source. A triumphant Vanderbilt set his price at $285 per share. Vanderbilt made $25 million, and after several corrupt legislators were thrown into personal bankruptcy, he had the great, albeit ironic, satisfaction of breaking up a most dishonest legislative body.

Vanderbilt's business philosophy was control and growth. He believed money was a means and not an end. To the Commodore, the goal was power and achievement. Unfortunately for the family fortune, Cornelius Senior didn't take the time to train his son and principal heir William Henry in these values.

William Henry Vanderbilt (1821–1885) increased the family fortune and became the richest man in the world. But although only one generation removed from the self-made Commodore, William Henry lacked the drive, the edge, the hunger necessary for empire building. He was more materialistic and concerned with protecting the fortune, rather than with expanding the empire.

Like his father, William Henry was a large man with strong features. His reddish sideburns were so outrageously overgrown that they fell over his collar and along his shoulders. William Henry had a passion for trotting horses, and in 1883 at New York's Fleetwood Park, he drove his famous pair of Aldine and Maud S. to a world record for the mile.

Vanderbilt's other avocation was collecting art. He traveled extensively in Europe in search of landscape and animal pictures. He didn't like

Impressionism, which was so popular at the time, and he wouldn't even look at nude paintings.

He jammed his Fifth Avenue mansion with paintings to such an untasteful extent that the result was a hodgepodge.

In an attempt to diversify family wealth, William Henry sold large blocks of stock in Vanderbilt railroads. He invested in safe government securities and railroad bonds. When he retired in 1883, his interest and dividend income amounted to more than $10 million per year. And when he died in 1885, he held $73 million in government bonds, plus $22 million in railroad bonds and $2 million in mortgages and other paper.

His entire estate was nearly $200 million, and most of it was bequeathed to his two oldest sons, Cornelius Vanderbilt II ($67 million) and William Kissam Vanderbilt ($65 million). Lesser sums of $10 million were given to each of William Henry's four daughters and two other sons, Frederick William and George Washington II.

Even though the family still controlled most of the Commodore's railroad empire, control had been split and therefore diluted. Although Cornelius II and William Kissam (known as Willie K.) assumed the chairmanships of the major railroads in the Vanderbilt system, management of the railroads was ceasing to be family business. Bankers like J. Pierpont Morgan and professional managers played an increasingly important role in the operations. Also, the two young railroad barons were not as intense or single-minded about the business as William Henry or the Commodore.

The two brothers had little in common. Cornelius II spent a great deal of time on charities and church activities, while Willie K. developed the lifestyle of a Gilded Age jet-setter, indulging in the leisure time activities of the born-rich.

After William Henry's death, the fabric of the Vanderbilt family began gradually to unravel. With the wealth dispersed and control of the railroads diluted, Vanderbilt interest and attention focused on a variety of diversions, and rifts and animosities erupted between family members.

The three principal schisms centered on that old nemesis: marriage and divorce in contravention to family wishes. The most controversial was the marriage of Cornelius III to Grace Wilson. Lesser controversies revolved around Frederick's marriage to Louise Torrance and Alva Smith's divorce of Willie K. and her subsequent remarriage to Perry Belmont.

The Commodore's heirs failed to create a dynasty like the Rockefellers, the Du Ponts, or the Fords. They lost control of the railroad empire and lacked the drive to regain or rebuilt it. They became aimless gentlemen spenders or financiers. Most viewed wealth as privilege and not something for constructive use. But blame must be shared collectively. The Commodore didn't take the time to pass his philosophy on to his son William Henry. William Henry in turn attempted to conserve capital and didn't understand the importance of building, and he never instilled in Cornelius II or in Willie K. the value of combining wealth with high purpose and personal abilities.

Also, the key Vanderbilt heirs (Cornelius II, Willie K., Frederick William, George Washington II, Cornelius III, Willie K. II, Alfred Gwynne, Reggie, and Harold) lacked the direction and the desire to build a dynasty, even though some accomplished much.

Cornelius Vanderbilt II (1843–1899) was the oldest son of William Henry and grandson of the Commodore. The Commodore intended for his grandson and namesake eventually to take over as head of the family and the railroad empire. He made certain that Cornelius II worked in the railroads and took a personal interest in his career.

The Commodore would probably not have wanted the empire split as it was in William Henry's will. But as William Henry diversified family wealth by selling railroad stocks, he also diversified family control by splitting power between his sons.

Cornelius II's lifestyle would probably not have pleased the Commodore either. The old man would have no use for Cornelius's penchant for charitable and religious activities. Cornelius donated much of his income and time to this effort; he was a Sunday school teacher and vestryman at his church.

Cornelius was a workaholic and diligently tackled his job with the railroads. When William Henry retired, Cornelius and Willie K. took over the chairmanships of the principal railways, with Cornelius getting the New York Central and the Michigan Central. So when William Henry died two years later, the brothers were firmly entrenched in the business.

Although Cornelius (and Willie K. to a lesser degree), was conscientious about family (meaning railroad) responsibilities, he lacked the intensity and vision necessary to build and preserve the empire. He depended heavily on banker J.P. Morgan and others for advice, even though their interests did not always coincide with those of the Vanderbilts.

Cornelius II was heavily involved in Newport life, principally as a pillar of the community. Yet, ironically, he is best known for creating The Breakers, a mansion that clashed so much with his phlegmatic personality.

A stern, solemn, seemingly ascetic man (didn't smoke or drink), Cornelius wasn't given to frivolity. He shunned society in favor of Sunday school. For Cornelius, The Breakers was the ultimate paradox. It was by far the most lavish and ostentatious private residence in Newport, if not the world. The only reasonable explanation for this incongruity lies with **Alice Claypoole Gwynne**, Cornelius' wife.

By the late 1880s, Alice Vanderbilt entered into a bitter rivalry with Alva Vanderbilt (Willie K.'s wife) for social dominance of the Vanderbilt family. The indomitable Alva had Alice outgunned when it came to manipulation and maneuvering, but as the wife of the head of the Vanderbilt family, Alice was not about to capitulate. And her ace in the hole was The Breakers.

In 1892, Cornelius Vanderbilt II selected the prolific and prominent architect Richard Morris Hunt to design a stunning mansion on

Newport's Ochre Point at the edge of the cliffs. Ironically, Hunt had designed Marble House for Willie K. and Alva. But The Breakers was his greatest achievement.

Certainly Hunt must have consulted extensively with Alice, since The Breakers, with its breathtaking opulence, was so out of character for Cornelius.

Hunt chose the style of European Renaissance and modeled The Breakers after a Northern Italian villa.

This imposing palace stands on the edge of the Atlantic Ocean overlooking the pounding surf.

Amazingly, Hunt took only two years to built The Breakers. The project was a tremendous undertaking, and included a workforce of hundreds of laborers and craftsmen, many imported from Europe. The logistics involved the selection and transportation of materials from Europe and Africa as well as coordination and collaboration with several noted architects and artists.

In France, craftsmen assembled (down to the last detail) the Grand Salon, which was then disassembled, crated, and shipped to Newport. Then, to ensure perfection, the same French craftsmen traveled to Newport and reassembled the room in The Breakers.

Cornelius Vanderbilt II (1843-1899)

47

In construction, Hunt used steel beams, stone, brick, and tile; but fearing fire (the old wooden Breakers had recently burned to the ground), he used no wood. With fire still in mind, Hunt segregated the furnace several hundred feet from the house, and connected it with a massive tunnel.

For the interior, he imported marble, alabaster, and stone from Italy, France, and Africa.

The entrace is guarded by enormous, but perfectly balanced oak doors. Weighing many tons, they still move at the slight push of a finger. Behind the oak doors, between the vestibule and the entrance hall, are a pair of huge hand-wrought, iron-grilled doors panelled with plate glass and weighing over seventy tons.

The Great Hall in the center of the mansion is awesome. It rises forty-five feet, and its majestic magnificence is numbing. The Great Hall rises through two full floors to a ceiling painted to look like a blue cloud-dotted sky. Carvings and marble plaques adorn the walls faced with French Caen stone. Huge fluted pilasters decorate the perimeter, and carved acorns and oak leaves (the Vanderbilt symbol) abound. The rooms on the second floor open onto balconies overlooking the Great Hall.

A grand circular staircase, with fountain beneath, divides at a landing and rises gracefully to a balcony. A huge (twenty-four by eighteen feet) Flemish tapestry overlooks the landing.

The Breakers Grand Salon, c. 1900

The billiard room, made of pale-green Cippolino marble from floor to ceiling, is trimmed in mahogany and contains an English weighing chair that gives the weight of the sitter in stones.

The most lavish and ornate is probably the dining room. A ceiling painting of Aurora at Dawn overlooks this spacious two-story room, which is surrounded by twelve massive red Numidian marble columns. Two huge chandeliers hang from a ceiling containing life-size figures set into arches.

The outside of this 17th-century stone palace exhibits double loggias (open galleries) with different-size arches, ornamental marble columns, and a variety of towers and terraces. The renowned Olmsted firm of landscape architects designed the grounds.

The house has seventy rooms, with thirty-three for the servants on a hidden fourth floor.

The breathtaking opulency and sumptuous ornamentation is saturating to the senses, and it is difficult to imagine anyone living comfortably in this overwhelming atmosphere.

But this was the home of Alice of The Breakers, and she clearly had the title of the biggest and best. In his memoirs, her grandson, Cornelius Vanderbilt IV, describes The Breakers and his grandmother:

> Downstairs, the kitchen was the size of a small house, with five immense wood-burning ranges, each with eight or ten burners. The butler's pantry was two decks high, and lined to the ceiling with fine glassware and china, all chosen from samples brought to Mrs. Vanderbilt's house, for it was said she had never entered a shop. At The Breakers she could give a dinner party for two hundred, it was rumored, without calling in extra help. And each morning, Mrs. Vanderbilt, wearing immaculate white gloves, inspected her household, running a gloved finger over table tops and picture frames and stair railings. And when she was through, the gloves had better be white!

Cornelius Vanderbilt II died in 1899 at age fifty-six. Many said he worked himself to death with worry and intensity over the railroads, numerous charities, and family responsibilities. Most people were unaware of the extent of his charatable involvement (he was a director of several large charities). Messages of condolence flowed in steadily for months.

Cornelius was a kind man, beloved by nearly everyone, but ironically he seemed unhappy and incapable of enjoying his vast wealth. And despite all his kindness, he sadly refused to reconcile with his eldest son, Cornelius Vanderbilt III (Neily), who had irrevocably angered his father by marrying the "wrong woman."

Even though Cornelius II spent and gave away vast amounts of his fortune, he still managed to increase his initial inheritance. His estate amounted to almost $73 million. Alfred Vanderbilt (second son) received the bulk of the estate (almost $43 million). Neily, his eldest, was virtually cut out; his share was $1,500,000.

Alice of The Breakers inherited a $7 million trust fund, and, of course, she got The Breakers. The other four children shared the rest of the estate.

Cornelius II clearly wanted Neily disowned, for the will specified that, if Alfred died, the estate would go to brother Reggie, and that if Reggie died, it would be shared by the girls.

However, after Neily threatened litigation, Alfred granted him an additional $6 million.

After her husband's death, Alice of The Breakers settled into the role of family matriarch. She never fully mended the rift with Neily or his wife, the strong-willed Grace Wilson Vanderbilt., But occasionally Alice attended balls at their Newport mansion, Beaulieu.

Alice had a long reign at The Breakers, and became an institution in Newport's social scene. She died in 1934 at age 89. The Breakers is now owned by the Preservation Society of Newport County and is open for public viewing.

Alice of the Breakers with daughter Gladys, 1907

Frederick William Vanderbilt (1856–1938) was the third son of William Henry Vanderbilt. Frederick, after graduating from Yale, spent most of his time immersed in the operation of the Vanderbilt railroads, and he was more prepared for the business than were any of his brothers.

However, when William Henry died, he left Frederick only $10 million and no real control over the Vanderbilt railways. Frederick angered his father when he married (in 1878) against his wishes. Louise Torrance was twelve years older than Frederick and divorced from his first cousin. But the headstrong and handsome Frederick (he had a handlebar mustache and slicked-down hair parted in the middle) married her anyway. Louise Torrance came from a reputable but only moderately well-off family. She was known as one of the great (but pampered) beauties of New York, and she longed for the grand lifestyle. William Henry was furious, but this fury boiled beneath the surface and was only completely apparent after the will was disclosed.

Having been shut out of the Vanderbilt super fortune, Frederick turned to banking and investments. In this arena he was a financial genius, and he multiplied his $10 million into an estate worth $76 million.

Frederick was not a big spender, and compared to other Vanderbilts, his tastes were simple. However, he had several houses and yachts, and he often kept a million dollars in his checking account. His mansion at Hyde Park, New York, is now a national historic site run by the federal government. He also had mansions in Newport, Florida, and Bar Harbor, Maine, and a Japanese fishing camp in the Adirondack Mountains.

Like so many other barons of the Gilded Age, Frederick was a reserved introvert and not caught up in the social whirl that so captivated his wife. During parties, he would often slip out the side door of the mansion to wander the grounds for hours.

In 1890, Frederick began building Rough Point, his massive stone mansion at Newport, and Louise entered a career of lavish entertainment. Rough Point sits near the bottom of Bellevue Avenue, atop the rocky cliffs overlooking the ocean.

However, Newport life bored Frederick, and by 1895 he began work on his Hyde Park estate. Later, he divided his time between Newport, New York, and cruising on his various yachts.

In his will, Frederick (he had no children) divided his fortune between several charities and his wife's relatives (with a large share left to Louise's niece, Mrs. James Van Alen). In the will, his festering anomosity toward the family for being denied control of the railroads surfaced. No Vanderbilt was left a penny.

George Washington Vanderbilt II (1862–1914), the youngest son of William Henry, showed little interest in railroads or high society. George used his $10 million inheritance to establish an enormous barony in the North Carolina mountains.

He bought about 125,000 acres and hired the eminent architect Richard Morris Hunt to design the Biltmore, a huge French Renaissance chateau. The ostentatious mansion, built in 1895, has 250 rooms (including 40 bedrooms), a 75-foot-high medieval banquet hall, and library space for 25,000 volumes. He employed the master landscape architect Frederick Law Olmsted (who designed Central Park and worked on several Newport mansions) to lay out the grounds. The Biltmore was a self-sufficient fiefdom with 750 employees working on farms, forestry projects, or in the estate's private village. Nearly the entire Vanderbilt clan travelled in private railroad cars to spend the Christmas of 1895 at the Biltmore.

After a few years as a country baron, George tired of the Biltmore estate and went tiger hunting in India. George was an eccentric intellectual who repudiated high society and business. He would much rather study ancient Greek and did, translating several contemporary works into that classic language. When he died in 1914, George was a poor Vanderbilt, and other than real estate and a $5 million trust fund, he had only $900,000.

William Kissam Vanderbilt (1849–1920), after inheriting an enormous sum, settled down to a life of serious leisure. In 1886, he built the fabulous yacht *Alva*. At 285 feet, she was the largest and most expensive ($500,000) private ship in the world. The three cabins on the main deck were steel plated and paneled with teak on the outside and mahogany on the inside. Willie K.'s personal quarters consisted of nine rooms. The dining room was 32 feet by 18 feet, with nine-foot ceilings, a fireplace, a piano, a skylight, and two brass chandeliers. The 16 feet by 18 feet library was paneled in French walnut and had its own fireplace and skylight. The *Alva* carried a crew of fifty-three, including a doctor.

In 1887, Willie K. took his wife Alva and their children on extensive cruises to the Caribbean, Europe, and the Middle East. Willie K. brought several friends, including the handsome and charming bachelor, O.H.P. Belmont.

Perry Belmont spent much time alone with Alva while Willie K. was off on his frequent and inexplicable side trips. This was an obvious precurser to eventual problems, since a few years later Alva shocked society by divorcing Willie K. and marrying Perry Belmont.

By the late 1880s, Willie K. was spending increasingly less time on New York Central Railroad business. Instead, his attention was on social diversions and playing the role of amiable clubman.

Along with the other leaders of New York society, Willie K. and Alva began spending their summers in Newport. Some of the Commodore's daughters had been regular summer visitors in the city, but they had not dominated its social life as later Vanderbilt matrons would. Even old William Henry was remembered for driving his trotters around Newport's streets.

Alva was determined to play a leading role in high society, and Willie K. promoted this effort in 1888, when he commissioned Richard Morris Hunt to build a marble palace near the cliffs on Newport's Bellevue Avenue.

Marble House opened in 1892 and secured for Newport the leadership of the American Renaissance in classical architecture. Patterned after the Trianon at Versailles, this most sumptuous residence (which still stands and is now a museum) has an imposing two-story entrance portico supported by gigantic fluted Corinthian columns. The ornate entrance grille weighs over ten tons. The entrance hall rises over twenty feet and is lined with yellow Italian marble. Throughout the house, the ornamentation is abundant with scenes and figures from Greek and Roman mythology. The rooms contain a variety of styles. The elegant dining room is faced with dark Numidian marble from Africa. And the Gothic Room and the rococo-style library contrast sharply with the Gold Room, which is a stunning display of gilt.

In 1893, the William K. Vanderbilts took another ocean voyage aboard Willie K.'s new yacht, the *Valiant* (the *Alva* had sunk after a collision near Martha's Vineyard). With seventeen-year-old daughter Consuelo and Perry Belmont among the guests, they departed for India on what was to be their longest and last cruise together.

In her memoirs, Consuelo Vanderbilt recalls the dreadful cruise as a series of "continual disagreements" and shouting matches between her parents. The cruise ended in a final blowout at Bombay, India. Willie K. and Alva hastily left the yacht and headed to Paris. Soon, Alva took the children to England and then back to Newport, in the fall of 1894. Willie K. stayed in Paris, and rumors described liasons with a beautiful Parisian lady. He already had an established reputation for philandering. When he returned to New York, he stayed at the Metropolitan Club, and visited Newport only for a few days to pick up his personal effects from Marble House.

Alva quickly filed for divorce, and in March of 1895, she became the first prominent American socialite to divorce her husband.

After the divorce, Alva waged a successful war against the Vanderbilt family and other socialites who attempted to ostracize her from society. In the face of severe slurs on her reputation, anyone with a weaker personality than the indomitable Alva could not have maintained her position in society. But her position in the Great Triumvirate was ironclad, and any matron who valued her social future wisely attended Alva's first ball that following summer at Marble House.

Although the Vanderbilt family refused even to acknowledge her existence, their efforts were futile, as Alva counterattacked, claiming she was the first society woman with nerve enough to divorce her husband (although many others would like to), and she threatened to blackball anyone siding with the Vanderbilts.

Alva was awarded Marble House in the divorce settlement, and in the summer of 1895, she held a fabulous ball for five hundred guests. The guest of honor was the young ninth Duke of Marlborough, Alva's hand-picked choice for daughter Consuelo's husband. Alva and Consuelo received guests admidst the luxurious dark pink Numidian marble of the dining room.

It was an extravagant floral fete featuring elaborate decorations of water hyacinths, lotus flowers, and swarms of live hummingbirds, butterflies, and bees. Nine French chefs prepared a sumptuous feast, with one course consisting of 400 mixed birds. The favors were Louis XIV-style fans, watch cases, and mirrors — all hand made in Paris and each bearing the Marble House medallion. The oriental silk lanterns that hung all over the grounds were hand made in China.

After intense negotiations, Consuelo and the Duke were betrothed. It was a significant social coup for Alva, but it cost Willie K. plenty. The frail and fragile Consuelo would become the ninth Duchess of Marlborough, princess of the Holy Roman Empire, and mistress of Blenheim Castle, but the Duke would get $2,500,000 in railroad stock, plus an annual allowance of $100,000.

The wedding was a spectacular ceremony at St. Thomas Episcopal Church in New York. The interior of the huge church was festooned with flowers top to bottom, and a sixty-piece orchestra played classical music. It was Alva's moment of glory; she had brought the Vanderbilt family into the upper crust of British nobility. However, revenge was sweet: except for Willie K. and Consuelo's brother, no Vanderbilt was invited to the ceremony.

Willie K. briefly increased his involvement in the railroads after brother Cornelius II, who had been extremely active, suffered a debilitating stroke in 1896. After Cornelius's death, in 1899, Willie K.'s interest in the railroads waned, and he bought an estate in France and began breeding race horses.

Willie K. spent most of his time in France with his horses, and just before he died, in 1920, he was the richest Vanderbilt alive. He died at age seventy-one, an intelligent, gentle man with no high purpose or direction in his life.

Yet, he still had loads of money. Even though he gave away $17 million in the last few months before his death (including $15 million to daughter Consuelo), he left a $55 million estate. His two sons, Willie K. and Harold Stirling, each received $21 million.

It is not entirely clear why Cornelius II so greatly abhorred the marriage of his son **Cornelius Vanderbilt III** to Grace Wilson.

Grace Wilson was the daughter of a prominent southern railroad baron. The Wilsons had later moved north to New York and established a significant social reputation.

Grace was three years older than Neily, and had an earlier but fleeting fling with his older brother. She also had been engaged to an English nobleman.

Maybe Cornelius could sense a certain shallowness or cold conceit in Grace, for she certainly cultivated a persona that would have repulsed the old puritan had he lived long enough.

The Vanderbilt family put on a full court press to scotch the marriage. But in the end, a headstrong Neily, after much anguish, married Grace anyway.

Grace Wilson Vanderbilt had a sweet tooth for high style, and the higher the better. Not that most other Vanderbilts didn't, but Grace's haughtiness and single-minded devotion to her role in the high caste were of an order of magnitude greater than those of most of her contemporaries.

Like many other socialites, she was enamored of Europe and its royalty. She traveled extensively on the Continent and competed

Grace Wilson Vanderbilt

intensely for royal attendance at her affairs.

She aspired to and attained the highest level of social leadership. In her Newport cottage, Beaulieu, and her Fifth Avenue mansion, she had probably the longest reign of anyone as queen of American society. It was estimated that in her heyday she entertained as many as 37,000 guests in one year.

Although there was some overlap of time, she didn't compete continuously with either Mrs. Astor or the Great Triumvirate, for her halcyon years were mostly after their's.

Grace reeked of self-importance and pomposity and had no use for social climbers, those who sought to attain what she had as a birthright.

Grace was a great friend of Alice Roosevelt Longworth, a noted raconteur and the daughter of President Teddy Roosevelt. Alice caused considerable controversy when, while Grace's house guest, she danced the "hootchy-kootchy" on the roof of Beaulieu.

The Beaulieu estate, which adjoins Alva Vanderbilt Belmont's Marble House, was the setting for several sumptuous balls. Possibly the most famous was the *Fete des Roses*, a lavish production that transplanted an entire Broadway cast and set to the shores of Newport.

The affair was so overwhelming that party guest Grand Duke Boris of Russia exclaimed, "Is this really America or have I landed on some enchanted isle? Such an outpouring of riches! It is like walking on gold."

In his book, Grace's son recalls that night in the summer of 1902 when she stood on the lawn welcoming her guests "standing in a little green circle of light, looking like a portrait by Gainsborough in her . . . pale-green and white gown and huge plumed black picture hat. With the costume she wore her cabochon emeralds and diamond stomacher. Directly behind her on the lawn of Beaulieu stretched a midway some 275 feet long, enclosed in turkey-red calico and blazing with red calcium lights looking, as one guest observed, like a 'tunnel of fire.' At the entrance to the midway stood a large jar of orchids and a Persian rug."

Glowing fairy lamps and big baskets of red roses were scattered copiously throughout the estate. Gold and silver fireworks sprayed over the cliffs and the moonlit ocean.

Scores of carpenters and craftsmen built a wooden theater on the lawn for a one-night stand of the Broadway hit, *Red Rose Inn.* The entire cast (including stars Irene Bentley and Eddie Foy), scenery, lights, props, and stage crew were brought in from New York. The theater on Broadway closed for two nights.

Confirming its exclusivity, only one hundred couples were included in the rarefied air of this enchanted evening.

After the play, dinner lead to dancing (two orchestras) into the wee hours, and the whole affair was capped by a sunrise breakfast.

Cornelius III (Neily) was the antithesis of Grace, and one wonders what they saw in each other.

Neily was frail, sickly, and introspective, in sharp contrast to Grace, the overbearing and regal socialite. His sharp facial features were exaggerated by a pointy goatee.

Neily, after being cut out of his father's will, developed a career with the family railroads. He became a prominent locomotive designer and engineer. Although he worked at the Vanderbilt railroads, he was not involved in senior management and had little contact with his estranged family.

He was an avid yachtsman, owning one of the most luxurious yachts afloat, the steam yacht *North Star,* and he became Commodore of the New York Yacht Club.

Possibly to escape from Grace and her social whirl, he joined the New York National Guard and fought in the Mexican War and in World War I, rising to the rank of Brigadier General.

Grace traveled extensively in Europe, giving parties everywhere. Most of the trips were without Neily, and as their incompatibility increased, they gradually drifted apart.

Grace was relentless in her pursuit of social dominance. Her parties were known as the most lavish around, and everywhere she went she was the most richly dressed. Jewelry abounded, often including a dog collar of pearls high around her neck and a large diamond dangling from a rope of pearls cascading across her bosom.

Between Newport and Fifth Avenue, the Vanderbilts entertained nearly every dignitary and big-wig around, from General Pershing to the Prince of Siam. This continued year in and year out as Grace marshalled an army of servants and a seemingly infinite bankroll to lock up the title of society's queen. In this process she managed to deplete an enormous portion of the Vanderbilt fortune.

Her social secretary met with her each morning to plan the details of future extravaganzas. She never saw any visitor who didn't have a pedigree as long as Fifth Avenue.

Grace and Neily's Newport mansion, Beaulieu, was built in 1859 for the Peruvian ambassador, Frederick de Barreda. Later, it was owned by William Waldorf Astor, who eventually sold it to Neily.

The cottage sits along Cliff Walk, overlooking the ocean. It is a massive but charming brick mansion. The house rises in perfect symmetry above a spacious terrace. The house is capped by a high concave French roof. The mansion gives the impression of dignity and power, but in a much more understated manner than the giant stone palaces and castles of Bellevue Avenue and Ochre Point.

The likes of Grace Wilson Vanderbilt would have been better suited to the sumptuous Marble House or The Breakers, but Neily's net worth, although formidible, was nowhere near the magnitude of Willie K.'s or the late Cornelius II's.

Nevertheless, Grace made it clear that her summer cottage was as significant and resplendent as anyone's. To do this she employed a French chef, an English butler, and assorted maids, nursemaids, and footmen. She maintained seventeen different vehicles and thirty horses, along with fifteen stable boys and a coachman. The children were left to an English governess while Grace entertained and was entertained.

The Vanderbilt's English butler, Stanley Hudson, was an imposing figure in the Beaulieu household. He changed his outfit three times a day and, except for his black vest, he was dressed just like Mr. Vanderbilt in the evening.

Next to the mistress and master, the butler held the highest rank in the household. And a good English butler could play this role to perfection.

Hudson never opened the front door or answered the telephone; footmen would do this. He wouldn't set the table, serve meals, pour wine, or wash dishes; footmen, again.

Hudson did greet guests, and, speaking in the third person, he would say, "If Madame will please be seated I shall see if Madam is in."

Grace's penchant for parties sometimes backfired. On one occasion, indignant Beaulieu servants staged a mild mutiny when Grace entertained the German ambassador at the outset of World War I.

It was the summer of 1914, Newport's last great social season, and the German army was rolling into Europe. Although the United States was not yet directly involved, there was heavy anti-German sentiment, particularly among the servant corps, which was profusely populated by French, English, and Belgians.

But Grace had such a strong affinity for European royalty, and she greatly admired the Germans. So, early in the summer, she planned a huge August celebration for the dashing German ambassador to Washington, Count Bernstorff.

Neily, who, at the time, was a lieutenant colonel in the New York National Guard, was outraged. He railed at the idea and scolded Grace severely: "She ought to be ashamed to be entertaining the German ambassador when her many French and English friends were engaged in such a terrible war and her two English nephews were in frontline trenches."

But even in the face of this stiff opposition, Grace was steadfast, the party would proceed.

After all, hadn't she entertained the Kaiser's brother in 1902 at her Fifth Avenue mansion, and hadn't she feted the Kaiser himself in 1903 aboard the Vanderbilt yacht *North Star* in the Bay of Naples? No no, the party would proceed.

So Cornelius Vanderbilt summarily announced that he would exclude himself from any affair honoring the Prussian Count.

Despite the obvious indelicacy of the situation and the uneasiness of all the guests, the count appeared on schedule and sat down to a tense dinner.

With the count seated at the place of honor on her right side, Grace presided over an uneventful first course. After the footmen served soup in white Sevres plates bordered in blue and gold, they left for the kitchen to get the fish course.

When the fish failed to arrive on time, Grace dispatched her butler to the kitchen to ascertain the cause of this breach in schedule.

When the butler didn't return, Grace grew increasingly tense. Now they were way behind, and Grace was a stickler for the schedule. An eight course dinner better be served in an hour flat or the servants would risk her wrath.

After several minutes, a kitchenmaid of a neutral nationality (probably Irish or Swiss) apprehensively appeared with a note on a silver tray. It was from the insubordinate servants: "We the undersigned regret to inform you, Madam, that we cannot any longer serve the enemy of our respective countries. We have thrown the rest of the dinner into the dustbin and we have all left your service. There is nothing else to eat in the house. We hope you all enjoyed the soup, for we took good care to spit well into, every one of us, before it went to the table."

The queasy guests reeled from the table after Grace read the message aloud. But after a brief recovery, the guests decided to prepare their own meal, and greatly enjoyed themselves amid the ensuing festival atmosphere.

Consistent with Newport's cachet, the servants returned the next day, and nothing further was mentioned by employer or employee.

Several other colorful Vanderbilts were closely connected to the Newport scene.

Alfred Gwynne Vanderbilt, Cornelius III's (Neily's) brother, benefitted from Cornelius II's animosity toward Neily and inherited the bulk of their father's fortune.

Alfred's interests were diverse and encompassed nearly all gentlemanly pursuits, particularly horses and motorcars. He owned the vast Oakland Farm outside Newport and was an avid horseman. At Oakland Farm, he built the largest exercise ring in the United States.

Alfred was the most handsome in this fourth generation of Vanderbilts. Slender, with pleasing features, he had the look of a movie star.

Alfred and Neily never fully bridged the rift between them. They would merely nod and rarely speak when they met on Bellevue Avenue or at the Reading Room.

Alfred's first wife, Elsie French Vanderbilt, divorced him in 1908 on charges of adultery. She accused him of sexual misconduct with the wife of a Cuban diplomat while aboard Alfred's private railroad car, the Wayfarer. The testimony of Alfred's valet was key to the settlement, which awarded Elsie French $10 million and custody of their son. The wife of the diplomat later committed suicide.

Alfred later married Bromo Seltzer heiress Margaret Emerson McKim. They had two sons, Alfred Gwynne II and George Washington III.

In 1915, Alfred and nearly 1200 others went down with the British liner *Lusitania* after a German submarine shot two torpedoes into her hull. There were several accounts of Vanderbilt's heroism in those moments.

Alfred's estate exceeded $26 million. His first son, fourteen-year-old William Henry III (who became governor of Rhode Island), received Oakland Farm, along with a $5 million trust fund.

Reginald Claypoole Vanderbilt was the younger brother of Neily and Alfred. Reggie owned another Newport farm, called Sandy Point.

Reggie was rotund and had a round, rather homely face. Reggie may not have had Vanderbilt looks, but he inherited more than a proportional share of Vanderbilt traits. He loved horses, gambling, wine, fast cars, and fast women.

After a disappointing stint at Yale, Reggie married Cathleen Neilson, a beautiful Newport heiress.

Reggie distinguished himself with a series of gambling debts, automobile accidents, and other unsavory acts of hard drinking and debauchery. In 1915, Reggie was fined for cheating on his income taxes.

In 1912, he deserted Cathleen and their daughter while on a trip to Paris. He left them high and dry with no money and no explanation. Eventually, Cathleen sued for divorce.

Reggie gambled extensively at Richard Canfield's casinos in New York and Newport. (Canfield's Newport gambling house is now a prominent restaurant, The Canfield House.)

When police raided the New York casino, they found $300,000 in I.O.U.s from Reggie.

Mrs. Reginald Vanderbilt (Cathleen Neilson) in 1913, deserted by her husband

Except for a $500,000 largess from brother Alfred's will, Reggie's cash flowed in one direction only, and by the early 1920s, high-living Reggie Vanderbilt had depleted a vast portion of his inheritance.

In 1923, Reggie married seventeen-year-old Gloria Morgan, the daughter of a prominent diplomat.

Alice of The Breakers (Reggie's mother) was so fond of Gloria that one evening when they were dining she ordered a scissors and, snipping off a third of her $200,000 string of pearls, handed them to Gloria. "All Vanderbilt women have pearls," she said.

For two wild years, Reggie and Gloria celebrated the Roaring Twenties. Between speakeasies, horse shows, and European trips, they had a baby, whom they named Gloria.

Then Reggie's lifestyle caught up with him, and he suffered a series of physical breakdowns. On doctor's orders, he swore off drinking and went to Vichy for the cure.

But the day he arrived back at Sandy Point Farm, Reggie went to the Reading Room and promptly got drunk.

Two weeks later, Reggie suffered severe internal hemorrhaging and died. After debts were settled, Reggie's estate consisted of nothing except his original $5 million trust fund.

His daughter Gloria was the center of a bitter custody battle that raged well into the 1940s. It pitted mother Gloria Morgan against aunt Gertrude Vanderbilt Whitney. Little Gloria had three husbands, including conductor Leopold Stokowski.

In 1899, **William K. Vanderbilt II**, the great grandson of the Commodore, was probably the most eligible bachelor in the country. Fresh out of Harvard, Willie K. II was a dapper, dark-haired sophisticate and the paradigm of the young adventurous millionaire.

But in 1899 he was a man in love, in love with Virginia (Birdie) Fair of Rosecliff, the heiress to a large portion of the Comstock lode. Although several years older than Willie K. II, Birdie was a vigorous and athletic young woman. A wedding was set for April.

The marriage melded two powerful families, and was masterminded by Alva Vanderbilt Belmont and Tessie Oelrichs, Birdie's older sister.

Willie K. II's father, the original William K. Vanderbilt, genuinely approved of the match, even though his ex-wife was the matchmater.

In the fall of 1899, the newlyweds took an extensive and hair-raising automobile trip through France. It was the early days of motoring, and conditions could be wild and woolly. They suffered several breakdowns and run-ins with the local culture as they careened through the countryside. The experience prompted Willie K. II to write what may have been the first guide for touring France by car.

The couple later purchased a villa in Newport and divided their time between New York, Europe, and Newport.

Willie's $21 million inheritance assured a life free from the burdens of work and financial problems.

In Newport, Willie spent a lot of time racing around in his autos. He was even fined for speeding along Ridge Road. Also, he's credited with saving fellow cottager Foxhall Keene after a canoeing accident off Bailey's Beach.

Throughout his life, Willie was heavily absorbed in adventurous hobbies. He was a complete automobile aficionado. He and Birdie took several motoring trips through Europe. Willie delved into auto racing and even set records. He participated in the grueling 1903 Paris to Madrid auto race. Officials finally stopped the race after fifteen contestants were killed. In those days, racing was primitive with few safety precautions.

Like many Vanderbilt families, Willie and Birdie separated, (in 1910), and were eventually divorced.

Willie had little interest in Newport social life and later devoted much of his time to his huge Long Island estate.

After automobiles, Willie immersed himself in yachting. This wasn't just gentleman cruising, but heavy sailing on the high seas for extended periods. Willie explored the world and collected fish and assorted sea life for a museum he established at his Long Island retreat, Centerport.

When Willie died, in 1944, his estate was valued at $36 million. This was before the age of aggressive tax planning, and the state and federal governments took $30 million.

Willie K. II's younger brother, **Harold Stirling (Mike) Vanderbilt** was quieter and less flamboyant, but no less the sportsman. Mike had the handsome and proud look of a Vanderbilt, and was by far the family's most famous yachtsman.

Willie K., Senior, Frederick, and Cornelius III had financed and syndicated previous America's Cup defenses, but none had actually sailed in the revered event.

Mike Vanderbilt successfully defended the America's Cup three times, when he skippered his victorious J-Boats off the coast of Newport. In 1934, he performed masterfully aboard *Rainbow*, when his decision-making prowess overcame a 2–0 deficit and a technically superior British boat, the *Endeavor*. In 1937, realizing the existing defenders would be no match for *Endeavor II*, he single-handedly financed *Ranger*, an outstanding boat.

Mike helped frame the rules for contract bridge and invented a bidding system called the Vanderbilt Club.

In 1954, as a member of the New York Central Board of Directors, Mike witnessed the demise of Vanderbilt control over their railroad empire. In a bitter proxy battle for control of the railroad, Texas oil money prevailed over New York bankers; Clint Murchinson, Sid Richardson, and Robert Young (also of Newport) seized control of the corner office. Mike and the rest were out; it was the end of an era.

BARONS AND BARONIES

The domains of the barons of Newport are largely intact today. Most are private residences, but several are open for public viewing. The streets of Newport are a living museum of a fabulous era, and the explorer is rewarded with a fascinating tour.

The houses of Newport's Colonial leaders and merchant princes are found mostly near the center of the city, in the Historic Hill and Point sections. And most of the intellectual elite who inhabited Newport in the 19th century lived in the stately shingle-style mansions located in the upper Bellevue Avenue and Kay Street areas. But the mansions and castles of the Gilded Age millionaires are scattered throughout lower Bellevue Avenue and Ochre Point, along Cliff Walk, and around Ocean Drive.

Unfortunately, many of these marvelous relics have been demolished. The residences of such Newport barons as Harry Lehr, J.P. Morgan, and Harry Payne Whitney no longer exist. But fortunately so many others still stand that Newport is truly a unique preserve of American heritage.

The best place to start a Gilded Age tour is on that most famous street, Bellevue Avenue.

A STROLL DOWN BELLEVUE

Refer to map on inside back cover.

Lower Bellevue Avenue stretches southward from Memorial Boulevard toward the ocean, to the beginning of Ocean Drive. An explorer starting from the north end will pass the stately Newport Casino on the left and almost immediately encounter turn-of-the-century mansions.

The first is **Kingscote** (built in the mid-1800's), on the right side, just before Bowery Street. **William King** bought this house in 1863. King had made a fortune in shipbuilding, real estate, and the China trade. Shortly after buying the house, King went insane and spent his remaining years in a mental hospital. Control of the house passed to family members who named the house "Kingscote" (King's cottage) and added an additional wing in 1882.

In 1895, the British Ambassador to the United States rented Kingscote and used it as his summer residence. During this time, "summer embassies" were common in Newport. Cossack guards stood in front of Stone Villa, the Russian "summer embassy," just north of Kingscote.

Richard Upjohn, the founder of the American Institute of Architects, designed the original Kingscote, and the New York architectural firm of McKim, Mead and White designed the 1882 addition. Upjohn is well known for his Gothic Revival style and was responsible for several churches including Trinity in New York and Saint Mary's in Portsmouth, Rhode Island.

Kingscote

Gothic Revival Kingscote, with its asymmetrical and irregular exterior lines, trimmed gables and dormers, and frieze-bordered roof edges, presents a charming and romantic image. The Gothic windows, variety of external forms, and rich detail contribute to this picture. The best view of the house is from the weeping willow tree at the edge of the circular drive.

The interior contains many of the same Gothic Revival features found on the outside: arches, columns, intricate woodwork, and variety in the size and shape of rooms. The most ornate and unusual room is the McKim, Mead and White dining room with mahogany paneling, cherrywood floor, Tiffany glass-tiled walls, and cork ceiling. In 1972, the Preservation Society of Newport County inherited Kingscote and opened it to the public.

At the corner of Bowery Street is **Berkeley Villa** (also known as Bellevue House). This Colonial Revival mansion was built in 1910 for heiress **Martha Codman**. She later married singer and famous art collector **Maxim Karolik**, who was thirty years her junior. Karolik, who

Berkeley Villa, Maxim Karolik

63

grew up in Russia, claimed to have heard of only three American cities: Washington, New York, and Newport. He described his boyhood image: "I didn't know much about Washington and I thought there were indians in New York, but I did know one thing—that American millionaires spent their summers in castles in Newport." The couple spent twenty happy years in this house.

Elmcourt, built in 1853, is on the right side of Bellevue Avenue, opposite Berkeley Street. This Tuscan Revival villa was one of the first on the Avenue. The Duchess de Dino once lived here in the 1800's, but for most of the Gilded Age it was owned by Frank Work of New York.

Elmcourt

Next to Elmcourt is **Edna Villa** (1882-1883). Designed by McKim, Mead and White, this cottage, with its sweeping porches and diverse shingle patterns, is a fine example of "shingle style" architecture. The irrepressible **James Gordon Bennett** built Edna Villa for his sister, Mrs. Isaac Bell, Jr.

Berkeley House (1884-1885), on the corner of Berkeley Street, is a brick Queen Anne style cottage built by Stanford White for **Leroy King**.

Next is the **Baldwin House** (1877-1878), a huge Queen Anne Revival combining brick, clapboard, and shingles into a Tudor style, with timbered gables, a penetrating chimney, and extending piazzas. The spacious interior hall is richly paneled and vaulted.

On the right side of Bellevue Avenue, just before Dixon Street, is a massive stone mansion called **The Elms**. In 1901, Philadelphia architect Horace Trumbauer designed The Elms for coal baron **Julius Berwind**. Trumbauer modeled The Elms after the Chateau d'Argenson, an 18th century classical Franch chateau. The lavish interior decoration is the work of the renowned House of Alavoine of Paris.

Nouveau riche Berwind, the son of poor German immigrants, made his fortune through his own efforts. In 1874, Berwind with his three brothers established a coal mining company which later became the dominant supplier to the United States Merchant Marine and Navy. Coal

The Elms, E.J. Berwind

fueled the Industrial Revolution, and at one point the Berwinds owned 260,000 acres of coal land.

Although Berwind lived and worked in New York, he became a weekend commuter during the summer season, sailing on the Fall River steamer to Newport on Fridays and returning to New York on Sunday evenings. A servant staff of twelve to sixteen cared for the Berwinds in their summer "cottage." Usually the Berwinds entertained on a comparatively small scale, but the ball to inaugurate the opening of The Elms was a lavish affair. It was probably the most spectacular party of the 1901 season, with extensive floral decorations, three orchestras, 125 couples, and pet monkeys running through the lawn.

Following the French classical style, symmetry, balance, and clarity are essential characteristics of The Elms. The interior is exquisitely adorned with elegant objects of art, lavish ornamentation on the walls and ceilings, authentic Louis XIV and XV furniture, and splended paintings loaned by the Metropolitan Museum of Art.

The ornate ballroom with curved corners presents a pleasing, flowing feeling to the eye. The opposing mirrors are interesting with their endless mutual reflections.

The fabulous grand staircase is made of white marble and limestone. The bedrooms are small in comparison to their European counterparts—reflective of their use only during a short summer season.

The terrace, lawn, and sunken garden exhibit horticultural excellence in the variety of plantings and meticulous design.

Surprisingly, the servants quarters are a hidden third-story consisting of sixteen rooms.

Berwind's sister Julia last occupied the house until she died in 1961. Then the Preservation Society of Newport County purchased The Elms and opened it as a museum, preserved for public viewing.

De la Salle (1882-1884), the **William Weld** mansion, is directly across the avenue from The Elms. Famous architect, Dudley Newton, designed this granite Gothic-style castle.

De la Salle, William Weld

On the left, after Dixon Street, is **Wayside** mansion, the residence of Gilded Age raconteur and chief competitor of Harry Lehr, **Elisha Dyer**.

White Lodge, the home of **Lispenard Stewart**, is next in line. This elegant villa had a Nile-green ballroom and a beautifully paneled dining room ornamented with delicate Gothic scrolls.

New York lawyer Lispenard Stewart was the most sought after bachelor in Newport. Trim, courtly, and conceited, Stewart was the epitome of Gilded Age gallantry. However, Stewart met his match in the rich and beautiful Mrs. Henry O. Havemeyer, Jr. She created a tense scene at one of Alva Belmont's Marble House balls when, although escorted by him, she spent the entire evening gossiping with friends. Stewart maintained his cool but vowed never to talk to her again.

After White Lodge, one encounters the **C.C. Baldwin** house, inexplicably named **Chateau-Nooga** (1880-1881). Windows and timbers abound in this ornate structure which was also known as the "Chatter Box."

Just off Bellevue Avenue, on the corner of Narragansett and Spring, is **Oakwood**, the former **DeLancy Astor Kane** estate. The great oak trees complemented a beautifully landscaped grounds and gardens.

Rockry Hall is on the right, at the corner of Narragansett Avenue. This stone and shingle Gothic villa was built in 1848 for **Albert Sumner**.

The **William Osgood House** (1887) is across the avenue. This rough-cut granite house is now part of Salve Regina College.

Swanhurst is on the right side, on the corner with Webster Street. Scottish stonemason, Alexander McGregor, built this fascinating fortress. The fine masonry walls in this Tuscan Revival villa are entirely obscured by a layer of stucco. McGregor, who also designed Fort Adams, Perry Mill, and the Newport Artillery Building on Clarke Street, built Swanhurst in 1851 for Judge Swan. Swan's descendant, Sallie Whiting, gave the house to the Art Association of Newport, and for many years it was an important cultural center.

On each side of Hazard Avenue are two estates once belonging to the renowned Brown family, the benefactors of Brown University. First is the **Harold Brown Villa**, a Gothic house designed in 1894 by Dudley Newton—the English-style landscaping was done by the famed Olmsted firm, the designers of New York's Central Park. The nearby mansion was owned by **John Carter Brown**.

Harold Brown Villa

On the left side of the avenue stands **Chateau-sur-Mer**, a formidable but picturesque granite castle made in the Victorian style. It sharply contrasts (and pre-dates) the ornate palaces of Bellevue Avenue. Chateau-sur-Mer was the most substantial and impressive Newport "cottage" when it was built in 1852 (and enlarged in 1872).

The ballroom was the first of significance in Newport. In 1857, the *fete champetre*, given by owner **William Wetmore**, attracted an estimated 2500 guests. This event, which presaged the gala turn-of-century balls, was the entertainment "benchmark" for Newport after the Civil War.

The property line at one time extended to the ocean; the name Chateau-sur-Mer means castle-on-the-sea.

William Wetmore (the first owner) earned his wealth from the China trade. His son, **George Peabody Wetmore**, became a powerful politician as governor of Rhode Island and United States Senator (1895-1913).

The atrium-like central hall is the most striking feature of the house—rising 45 feet to a glass ceiling and skylight and surrounded

Chateau-sur-Mer, Wetmore family

by balconies on each floor. The Italian decorator, Frulini, designed much of the interior, such as the walnut library finely carved in Renaissance style. The carvings in the Frulini dining room extol the sensual pleasures of eating and drinking in Bacchic (god of wine) tradition.

Underneath the stairs, the painted Tree of Life rises three stories to a ceiling decorated with birds and a blue sky.

On the outside, the irregular Victorian lines, high mansard roof, and rough granite walls present a harsh, sharp appearance. The huge weeping beech across from the entrance, with branches touching the ground, gives an explorer the feeling of walking through a forest.

The daughters of George Wetmore, Edith and Maude, were leading Newport socialites and philanthropists. Edith Wetmore along with Mrs. John Jacob Astor, pioneered the game of women's tennis at the Casino when they daringly wore white tennis shoes, black stockings, white silk blouses, and pleated skirts with bloomers. The outfits were topped with sailor hats, over double veils to protect delicate faces from the summer sun.

Mrs. Richard Gambrill, an influential widowed socialite, reigned from the majestic **Vernon Court** (on the left, past Shepard Avenue). Designed for lavish entertainment, this French Provincial chateau was built in 1901 by architect Thomas Hastings, the designer of the New York Public Library. White stuccoed walls, heavily ornamented in terra-cotta, and an enormous multi-chimneyed roof are prominent features of this sophisticated structure. The grand formal grounds include a copy of Henry VIII's garden for Anne Boleyn.

At the turn of the century, Scottish multi-millionaire **I. Townsend Burden** owned **Fairlawn** (1852), an Elizabethan estate built of brick

Vernon Court, Mrs. Richard Gambrill

and brownstone. Fairlawn is just past Ruggles Street on the left side. Mrs. Burden was the first socialite to invite fellow Baltimorean Harry Lehr to Newport, thus launching a most bizarre social career.

In 1883, the estate was owned by Levi Morton, who was Vice President of the United States in the Benjamin Harrison administration and Governor of New York.

A little further down the avenue, on the left, one encounters the exquisite **Rosecliff** mansion, the former summer residence of **Mr. and Mrs. Hermann Oelrichs**. The New York architectural firm of McKim, Mead and White designed Rosecliff after the Grand Trianon Palace built by Louis XIV in Versailles.

From 1851 to 1891, George Bancrft—noted diplomat, historian, horseman, and horticulturist—owned the land now occupied by Rosecliff. Bancroft was the founder of the U.S. Naval Academy and Ambassador to England and Prussia. He is credited with establishing the extensive rose beds for which the property is named.

In 1891, Theresa and Virginia Fair purchased the Rosecliff property for $140,000. Theresa and Virginia (affectionately known as Tessie and Birdie) were the daughters of James Fair, an Irish immigrant who made a fortune by striking the largest vein in the Comstock Lode—one of the largest gold and silver deposits ever discovered. Later, Fair became a U.S. Senator from Nevada. Fair gave Theresa a million dollars when she married Hermann Oelrichs, a wealthy New York businessman. After he died, Fair's enormous wealth passed to his two daughters. Mrs. Oelrichs (Theresa) built the existing Rosecliff house from 1899 to 1900 and became one of the outstanding hostesses of Newport society.

Rosecliff is H-shaped with two partially enclosed terraces. The garden terrace, an 18th century French Court of Love, was patterned after one built for Marie Antoinette. The first floor, used for

Rosecliff, Mrs. Hermann Oelrichs

entertaining, is about twenty feet high, while the second floor (bedrooms) is only ten feet. The third floor is concealed and was used for servant's quarters. The outside is covered with white terra cotta—a fired clay that looks like stone.

The intention was entertainment—on a grand scale—as seen in the spacious first floor design. Rooms and doors are arranged to permit the smooth movement of many people. The most striking feature of the interior is the spectacular curving marble staircase, which gracefully flows in a heart-shaped fashion. Other notable features are the massive archway leading into the stair hall, and the walls and ceilings (particularly in the ballroom), which are extravagantly adorned with carved and molded plaster fashioned into rococo designs. The Rosecliff ballroom is the largest in Newport.

The south rose garden, restored in 1976, has paths paved with marble chips and contains 180 plants.

In 1973, scenes for the movie *The Great Gatsby* were filmed at Rosecliff.

Rosecliff is the property of the Preservation Society of Newport County and is open for public touring.

In the rarefied air of the strictly closed Newport society, the **Pembroke Joneses** were successful social climbers from North Carolina. Jones was a rice baron who rapidly penetrated High Society, after relocating to New York. The social gatecrashers set up housekeeping in the magnificent **Sherwood** mansion (1904), located on the right side of the avenue, opposite Rosecliff.

The Joneses overcame objections from Newport's Old Guard by throwing lavish Southern dinners and entertaining in a grand style. Mrs. Jones regularly earmarked $300,000 for entertainment at the beginning of each Newport season.

For one party, they thought nothing of building an 85 by 40 foot completely enclosed outdoor ballroom and theater, decorated with floor-to-ceiling plate glass mirrors and 10,000 water lillies.

Contrary to the social norms of Newport society, Pembroke Jones was always ready with a hearty laugh, a ribald joke, or a pre-lunch mint julep.

Sherwood is an expansive Georgian mansion, with a huge columned portico and several similarities to the "White House."

The fabulously wealthy Palm Beach real estate and hotel baron, Henry Flagler, met the love of his life, Mary Lily Kenan, while visiting Sherwood. In Cinderella tradition, Mary Lily was a poor relative of the Joneses and a shy recluse who spent her days upstairs sewing, until discovered by Flagler. As Flagler's young wife, she would later inherit an enormous sum and go on to become a most powerful and influential woman.

Sherwood, Pembroke Jones

Beechwood is located on the left side, opposite Bancroft Avenue. Beechwood was the home of **Mrs. Caroline Astor**, the queen of Newport society. This charming stuccoed brick house, with its spacious piazzas and breathtaking ocean view, was built in 1852. Beechwood is open to the public.

Adjoining Beechwood is **Marble House**, the magnificent **William K. Vanderbilt** mansion. Marble House is most famous for its former mistress, the indomitable **Alva Vanderbilt Belmont**, a full-fledged member of the Great Triumvirate and one of the most powerful American women of her time. Both Marble House and Alva Belmont are described in detail elsewhere in this book (see **The Great Triumvirate** and **The Vanderbilts**).

In apparent contradiction to its sunny name, **Champ Soleil** hides amidst the trees, on the right side. **Mrs. Drexel Dahlgren**, of the Main Line Philadelphia Drexels, built this profusely landscaped French Provincial estate in 1929.

Beaulieu mansion stands next to Marble House, on the edge of the sea. Beaulieu, built in 1859 for the Peruvian ambassador to the United States, has seen more than its share of Gilded Age barons. No

Beechwood, Mrs. Caroline Astor

Marble House

less than **James Gordon Bennett, William Waldorf Astor, General Cornelius Vanderbilt,** and **Grace Wilson Vanderbilt** made Beaulieu their summer residence. The haughty and overbearing Grace Vanderbilt threw legendary parties throughout her long stint at Beaulieu (see **The Vanderbilts**).

Beaulieu has a charming French concave (mansard style) roof, densely bricked walls, and a deep sea-side veranda.

Clarendon Court is next to Beaulieu. The architect of The Elms, Horace Trumbauer, designed this 18th-century English mansion in 1904. **Edward Knight**, an executive of the Pennsylvania Railroad, was the original owner, but Clarendon Court has seen several other barons, including **Maysie Rovensky**, whose son Philip Plant is remembered as the husband of actress Constance Bennett. It is alleged that Plant's lifestyle was responsible for the coining of the word "playboy." The Rovensky's bequeathed Rovensky Park—across the avenue from the mansion.

However, the most well known owners of Clarendon Court were surely **Claus and Martha "Sunny" von Bulow**. Claus was twice tried for attempted murder of his wife, after she lapsed into an irreversible coma resulting from insulin injections. He was convicted and then acquitted on appeal. After a lawsuit by Sunny's children, Claus agreed to give up his rights to Clarendon Court and her inheritance.

Adjoining Clarendon Court is **Miramar**, another Horace Trumbauer work. **Mrs. George Widener** of Philadelphia built Miramar in 1914. The mansion, set in extensive formal gardens, is a model of classical architecture and rigidity. In 1912, the year construction began on Miramar, Mr. Widener and his son perished on the *Titanic*. Later Mrs. Widener married noted explorer **Dr. Alexander Hamilton Rice**.

Miramar

Mrs. George Widener, Miramar

73

Balls at Miramar were legendary, particularly during Tennis Week. In the Newport tradition, they lasted all night, but Mrs. Rice would nap shortly after midnight and return just before breakfast to freshly greet the revelers.

Mrs. Widener was the donor of Harvard's Widener Library.

Opposite Miramar and a little further down the avenue is **Belcourt Castle**, the former home of **Oliver Hazard Perry Belmont** and his wife, **Alva Vanderbilt Belmont**.

This sixty-room castle, patterned after a Louis XIII hunting lodge at Versailles, contains the largest collection of 13th-century stained glass in America.

Antiques and art treasures abound in this eclectic museum. Oriental rugs (over 100), exquisite Renaissance furniture and paintings, and all sorts of armor and urns adorn the castle.

Oliver Hazard Perry Belmont built this castle (for about $3 million) in 1894, two years before he married the former Mrs. William K. Vanderbilt, the ex-mistress of Marble House. The new Mrs. Belmont was one of Newport's great hostesses, and Belcourt became the scene of many fabulous balls.

Oliver's father, August Belmont, established the family fortune in banking and later married the daughter of Commodore Matthew Perry, who was known for opening trade with Japan. Also, Oliver's grand uncle and namesake won the legendary Battle of Lake Erie.

August Belmont had a great interest in Thoroughbred horses, and part of his fortune went to build Belmont Park horse track in New York.

The Belmonts entertained extensively. Belcourt guests included the Duke of Windsor and Kaiser Wilhelm. Even lunch could be lavish, and Mrs. Belmont was known to invite friends from nearby Bailey's Beach back to the castle for a midday buffet banquet of lobster, ham, and turkey.

Belcourt Castle

The prominent architect of the times, Richard Morris Hunt, designed Belcourt and supervised construction over a three-year period.

The interior design of the castle reflects French influence, particularly from the 16th-century.

The Grand Hall, guarded by two imposing Italian marble columns, contains innumerable Chinese works of art and an 18th-century bronze statue of Apollo. Apollo appears again in the dining room driving his sun chariot along the ceiling. There's also indirect lighting designed by Belmont's friend, Thomas Edison.

The archetypical Gothic ballroom is an amalgamation of vaulting stained-glass windows and columns. The room contains an extensive armor collection, 15th-century German throne chairs, and a great fireplace that looks like a castle.

The exterior walls are 42 inches thick and built of brick and granite. Built for endurance, the Castle sits on a four-foot thick block of concrete.

Belcourt Castle is currently owned by the Tinney family, and they have opened their spectacular museum for public touring.

Ocean View, across from Belcourt, is a distinguished mansard-roofed wooden house built in 1866. During the Gilded Age, it was the home of **Mr. and Mrs. Ogden Mills**. The Mills were old line aristocrats who entertained in a formal, stately fashion. Mrs. Mills claimed she could give a party for a hundred without calling in extra help. But she was much too self-important and strait-laced to gain popularity among the more hedonistic Gilded Agers. Ogden Mills was Secretary of the Treasury during the Hoover administration.

Mr. and Mrs. Ogden Mills, Ocean View

Ocean View

Rough Point (1890) sits on the edge of the cliffs, above the pounding surf. This sandstone Tudor mansion, with its great Gothic hall and vast lawns, was the home of the immensely wealthy financier, **Frederick Vanderbilt**, the grandson of the famous Commodore.

Later in the Gilded Age, **Mr. and Mrs. William Leeds** lived in Rough Point. The nouveau riche Leedses (he was known as the Tinplate King) were initially shunned by the Old Guard of Newport society. But they later won the support of Alva Vanderbilt Belmont and secured their place at the pinnacle. The young, charming and beautiful Mrs. Leeds was to preside over many lavish balls at Rough Point.

Later, tobacco heiress and famous Newport restorer, **Doris Duke**, lived in Rough Point.

Rough Point is on the left side of the avenue, at the point where the road takes a sharp right turn. The estate is on a somewhat remote section of the cliffs and is further secluded from Bellevue Avenue by stone walls.

Rough Point

Mrs. William Leeds, Rough Point   *Doris Duke, Rough Point*

Roselawn is on the right side, as Bellevue Avenue takes a sharp right turn. **Mrs. J.F. Pierson** lived in this "carpenter Gothic" villa, with its multi-gabled roof and spacious porches.

Also on the right side, on the corner of Ledge Road, is **Inchquin**, a rough-cut granite French Renaissance villa.

On the left, all the way down Ledge Road toward the ocean, are two fine cottages situated at the end of Cliff Walk. **Land's End** (1890) was the home of novelist and Newport intellectual, **Edith Wharton**. The three-story, sixteen room stuccoed cottage sits on the left side of the road next to Cliff Walk. **The Waves** is on the other side. In 1927, architect **John Russell Pope** (Jefferson Memorial) built The Waves for himself. The rambling multi-gabled villa blends nicely with the surrounding rocks and ridges.

Land's End, Edith Wharton

The Waves, John Russell Pope

Beachmound is the last house on Bellevue Avenue. Built in 1897 for Pittsburg's **Benjamin Thaw**, this Colonial Revival mansion has a huge pillared portico and a great view of Bailey's Beach.

Beachmound, Benjamin Thaw

A WALK ALONG THE CLIFFS

Cliff Walk begins (on the north) at Memorial Boulevard, near Easton's Beach (First Beach). A walk along the entire span will yield spectacular views of the crashing surf on one side and fabulous Gilded Age mansions on the other.

A southward walker will pass a few notable cottages before arriving at Narragansett Avenue and Forty Steps.

Cliff Lawn (now called Cliff Walk Manor), one of the first great houses built on the cliffs, is on Memorial Boulevard overlooking First Beach. Cliff Lawn was the home of **Winthrop Chanler** and was the site of a christening party in 1902 for Chanler's grandson, which was attended by his godfather, **President Theodore Roosevelt.**

About a quarter of a mile down the winding walk is **Hopedene**, a Colonial Revival cottage built in 1902 for **Mrs. E.H.G. Slater** of Providence. The house is hard to see from the walk due to heavy vegetation—but it can be clearly viewed from Easton's point, on the opposite side of First Beach.

A little further is **Ocean Lawn**, a vast Queen Anne cottage with ornately carved Gothic gables, built for **Mrs. William Gammell** in 1889. This house is also difficult to see from the walk.

Southside, another Queen Anne cottage, is just past Narragansett Avenue and Forty Steps. Famous Gilded Age architects, McKim, Mead and White designed Southside (1882) for **Robert Goelet** of New York. This magnificent house is a fine example of shingle style construction. Intricately arranged shingles, upper-level galleries, a multi-chimneyed roof, and a broad piazza mark the exterior. The interior opens freely around a great hall fireplace.

In a storybook romance, Goelet's son Robert married Elsie Whelen, one of the poor but gorgeous Whelen twins. The willowy Elsie became a classic Newport belle—tall and dark with long flowing lines and the picture of grace in a ballroom. Gilded Age author Blanche Oelrichs describes these Newport belles: "How beautifully they stood

Southside

Mrs. Robert Goelet, Southside, 1911

and moved...with their evening dresses caught up under their breasts, wearing fresh gardenias in their hair, their slim throats encircled by necklaces of emeralds and sapphires." Alas, the couple soon divorced, and Elsie married Henry Clews of The Rocks.

The next summer cottage is the ornate **Ochre Court**, the former home of **Mr. and Mrs. Ogden Goelet**. Ochre Court is a fifty-room French chateau built in 1888 for Ogden Goelet, a wealthy New York real estate developer. Richard Morris Hunt modeled Ochre Court after Edward VII's castle in Paris. The design exhibits high roofs, turrets, and tall chimneys. Other exterior features include sandstone carvings of gargoyles and griffins.

The Great Hall in Ochre Court rises over two stories and is surrounded by an ornate balconied gallery. In 1947, Goelet's son Robert donated the mansion to the Catholic Diocese of Providence, and it is now part of Salve Regina College.

Author Blanche Oelrichs describes Ogden Goelet as a man who had worked himself to death. She recalls seeing Goelet shuffling around the grounds of Ochre Court on the arm of his nurse. She was told Goelet could digest nothing but grapes.

Mrs. Goelet, on the other hand, became a most pursued widow. Enormously rich, arrogant, and calculating, she lived in gilded splendor behind the gates of the magnificent Ochre Court. She entertained lavishly and is remembered as the hostess who battled Mamie Fish in the Grand Duke War (see **The Great Triumvirate**).

Ochre Court, Ogden Goelet

Vinland is next in line along the Walk. It's the former summer home of **Mrs. Hamilton McKown Twombly**, the last of the great Newport *grande dames*. Mrs. Twombly, the last grandchild of Commodore Cornelius Vanderbilt, presided over Vinland for more than fifty years, before she died in 1952 at the age of ninety-eight.

Vinland, built in 1883, is a brownstone Queen Anne villa with fifty rooms. The Boston architectural firm of Peabody and Stearns designed Vinland. At one point, the estate had more than fifteen automobiles, all painted in Vanderbilt maroon.

Mrs. Twombly's sumptuous dinners included the finest French *haute cuisine*, and her French chef became wealthy enough to retire in his own Newport cottage.

When she rode cross-country in her Rolls Royce to attend her grandson's wedding, Mrs. Twombly dressed as a maid and sat in front with the chauffeur, while her maid rode in the back disguised as the dowager.

Adjoining Vinland is **The Breakers**, the most fabulous and massive of all Newport mansions. The Breakers was built in 1892 by Richard Morris Hunt for **Cornelius Vanderbilt II**. Both the mansion and its occupants are described in detail elsewhere in this book (see **The Vanderbilts**).

Vinland, Mrs. H.M. Twombly

As Cliff Walk turns sharply to the right (west), **Anglesea** sits on the point with a commanding view of the ocean. It's a rambling stick-style cottage built around 1880.

The walk continues around Ochre Point, skirting **Fairholme**, enlarged in 1870 for **Fairman Rogers** from Philadelphia. Rogers was the author of the authoritative manual of coaching.

This large Tudor villa, with medieval half-timbered facade, was later owned by the Drexel family.

However, **Mr. and Mrs. Robert Young** were probably the most famous owners. Railroader Robert Young—of Newport, Palm Beach, and White Sulphur Springs—was the tycoon who wrested the reins of the New York Central from the Vanderbilt family. Mrs. Young often entertained the Duke and Duchess of Windsor at Fairholme.

A little further along the walk is **Midcliff** (1886), the former home of Oklahoma oil heiress, Minister to Luxembourg, and hostess *par excellance*, **Pearl Mesta**. She entertained Dwight Eisenhower and Hoover's vice president, Charles Curtis.

Midcliff is followed by **Honeysuckle Lodge** (1886), a rambling Queen Anne cottage and former home of famous golf enthusiast, **T. Suffern Tailer**.

The Breakers

Fairholme, 1931

EXPLORING OCHRE POINT

After Honeysuckle Lodge (at Marine Avenue), Cliff Walk continues southward for more than a mile. The walk gradually becomes more primitive and ends at Ledge Road. Most of the mansions along this section also border Bellevue Avenue and are described earlier. However, the oceanside perspective is rewarding and should not be missed.

There are several other mansions of interest in the general Ochre Point area (between Ochre Point Avenue and Bellevue Avenue).

Edson Bradley, a Washington liquor baron, built **Seaview Terrace** in the late 1920's. It's patterned after the French Renaissance style of a Norman manor house, with a soft-toned limestone exterior extensively adorned with cornerstones and cornices.

The house is located on Ruggles Avenue near Cliff Walk, just west of Honeysuckle Lodge.

Mr. Bradley filled his house with tapestries, stained glass, and an eclectic selection of art treasures. This fifty-four room mansion was the last great mansion built in Newport and contained a chapel which seated 150 people.

Seaview Terrace, Edson Bradley

In ironic ratification of changing times, Seaview Terrace cost over $2 million to build, but sold for only $8,000 in 1949. In the days before condominium conversion, the upkeep and taxes were too great a burden. Today, the house would obviously sell for millions.

The **Watts Sherman House**, located on Shepard Avenue near Lawrence Avenue, is a classic example of Queen Anne style. This Tudor manor house was built in 1874 for New York banker **William Watts Sherman**.

Exterior highlights are a stone first story below shingles arrayed in beautifully intricate patterns, bay windows, and half-timbering set in terra-cotta stucco. The exquisite interior has rich paneling, ornately carved woods, beamed ceilings, and La Farge stained glass.

Watts Sherman House

James Van Alen's former home, **Wakehurst**, is a fascinating copy of an English country manor house. At first glance, it seems almost a mini Elizabethan castle, as it lords over a beautifully landscaped estate, but it's really a charming stone Tudor mansion.

Van Alen was a railroad heir who married Mrs. Caroline Astor's daughter, Emily. After his wife died, Van Alen hoped to become the Italian ambassador, but crusading Joseph Pulitzer, publisher of the *New York World*, who had no use for the idle-rich Van Alen, scotched the appointment by printing a scathing editorial against Van Alen's lifestyle.

James Van Alen, handsome and elegant, was Newport's most eligible widower. But maybe most of all, he was a consummate Anglophile. He loved everything British and adorned Wakehurst with English tapestries, antique "period furniture," high-backed oak benches, dower chests, grandfather clocks, pewter tankards, etc. Eccentrically, Van Alen even flavored his vocabulary with such Tudor period expressions as "egad," "zounds," "varlet," and "wench."

Van Alen was firmly established at the upper crust of Newport society. He was a connoisseur of food and wine, and his musicales and parties were the height of fashion.

Wakehurst is now part of Salve Regina College.

Wakehurst, J.J. Van Alen

Miss May Van Alen,
granddaughter of Mrs. Astor

Set behind the trees at the east end of Narragansett Avenue, opposite Ochre Point Avenue, is an elegant French chateau known as **The Orchard**. The mansion was built in 1871 and is an exact copy, formal grounds and all, of an 18th-century French country house. During the Gilded Age the house was owned by **Colonel George Fearing**.

Traveling west on Narragansett Avenue, an explorer will soon encounter **Bois Dore**, one of the last great Newport mansions (1927). The design is decidedly 18th-century France for this huge limestone chateau built for Pennsylvania's **William Fahnestock**. Fahnestock was known for hanging 14-carat artificial fruit from the trees of the Bois Dore estate.

A RIDE AROUND THE DRIVE

The southern end of Bellevue Avenue is a good place to begin a tour of Ocean Drive. The Drive starts at Ocean Avenue, near Bailey's Beach, where Bellevue Avenue ends.

On the left, just past Bailey's Beach, is a stick-style cottage known as **The Ledges**. The rambling house, built in 1867 for **Robert Cushing**, has a commanding view of the ocean and the surrounding shoreline.

Ocean Drive Area

Newport Harbor

Fort Adams

Wellington Ave.

Narragansett Bay

Hammersmith Farm

Harrison Ave.

Harrison Ave.

Thames St.

Spring St.

Bellevue Ave.

Ruggles Ave.

Coggeshall Ave.

Ridge Rd.

Newport Country Club

Brenton Rd.

Hazard Ave.

Carroll Ave.

Castle Hill

Almy's Pond

Hazard's Beach

Gooseberry Beach

Bailey's Beach

Brenton Point Park

Ocean Ave.

Ocean Ave.

Price's Neck

Atlantic Ocean

William Miller's French chateau sits on the opposite side, high above the shore. The stucco and timber facade has the look of a fortress against a hostile environment. Miller appropriately named his house **High Tide** (1900).

Mrs. Stuyvesant Fish's Colonial mansion, **Crossways** (1898), was the scene of many famous social events. A member of Newport's Great Triumvirate, the outrageous Mrs. Fish was one of the most colorful socialites of the Gilded Age (see **The Great Triumvirate**). The mansion is on the right, just before Gooseberry Beach (see photo on page 42).

Idle Hour, a French Provincial manor house, is on the right side, opposite Hazard's Beach and overlooking Lily Pond. It was built in 1929 for **Mrs. Fredric Allen.**

On the left, past Hazard's Beach, is a series of magnificent oceanside cottages: **Nearsea** (1937), **Little Clifton Berley** (1930), **Eagle's Nest** (1924), **Normandie** (1914), **Seafair** (1937), **Bay House** (1917), **Play House** (1926), and **Wildacre** (1901). French and English architectural styles dominate this charming array of houses. Wildacre was the home of **Albert Olmsted**; the Olmsted brothers were the premier landscape architects of the Gilded Age.

Wildacre, A.H. Olmsted, c. 1900

Opposite Wildacre, up on a bluff, is a stone and shingle mansion designed by Richard Morris Hunt in 1891. The secluded **Wrentham House** blends harmoniously with the surrounding rocks and shrubbery.

Ocean Avenue winds past the venerable **Newport Country Club** (1894) on the right and around Brenton Point to Castle Hill.

The **Castle Hill House** (now the Inn at Castle Hill) was the home of **Professor Alexander Agassiz**, the renowned marine scientist and turn-of-the-century intellectual. The shingle mansion (1874) has a great view of the East Passage of Narragansett Bay.

Castle Hill House, Alexander Agassiz

Ocean Avenue runs into Ridge Road, which winds back toward Newport Harbor. Past the Coast Guard station, on the left side, is **Shamrock Cliff** (now Ocean Cliff), the former **G.M. Hutton** estate. The main house (1896) is patterned after an Irish country castle.

Hammersmith Farm is near where Ridge Road turns into Harrison Avenue. Hammersmith was built in 1888 for **John Auchincloss**. The shingle-style construction combines stone, brick, and wood in this classic 19th-century seaside cottage. The estate is open for public touring.

Hammersmith Farm, John Auchincloss

Just after Hammersmith, there's a small farmhouse near the entrance to Fort Adams. The farm was the setting for **Harriet Beecher Stowe's** novel, "The Minister's Wooing."

Beyond Fort Adams, overlooking Brenton Cove, is a classic Georgian mansion perched precariously on the rocks and looking like a Greek temple. McKim, Mead and White designed **Beacon Rock** in 1889 for **Edwin Morgan**. It is now owned by Felix de Weldon, scupltor of the Iwo Jima statue.

Edgehill, another McKim, Mead and White design, was built in 1887 for **George King**. The turreted stone and slate villa is on Harrison Avenue, before Beacon Hill Road.

After Edgehill, Harrison Avenue turns ninety degrees to the left and proceeds down to **Beachbound** (1895), a huge granite and shingle castle built by Peabody and Stearns for **William Burden**. The mansion is right on the water, with a great view of Newport Harbor.

Harrison Avenue turns sharply to the right and passes by **Bonniecrest** (1912-1918), a classic Tudor stone and brick manor house designed by John Russell Pope for **Stuart Duncan**. The landscaping was by the famed Olmsted brothers. Ironically, Bonniecrest, the scene of more than a few fabulous balls, resembles country manors in Worcestershire, England, and Mr. Duncan was chairman of Lea and Perrins, makers of Worcestershire Sauce (see photo on page 17).

Just past Bonniecrest, Harrison Avenue intersects Halidon Avenue, a short road leading down to the harbor. On the left, before the harbor and behind a stone wall, is **Harbour Court**, the former residence of **Mrs. John Nicholas Brown** of that famous Providence family. Harbour Court, built in 1904, is an enormous French chateau with a great view of Newport Harbor. The New York Yacht Club is the current owner.

Beacon Rock, Edwin Morgan